THE SYSTEM MADE ME DO IT!

A Life Changing Approach to Office Politics

by Susan M. Osborn, Ph.D.

To Karen & Bob
Very best wishes!
Susan
May 1997

LifeThread Publications

1997

LifeThread Publications
P. O. Box 185
Newark, CA 94560-0185
(510) 792-5295

First Edition
Printed in the United States of America
Text Design by Julia K. Osborn

Although the author has exhaustively researched all sources to ensure the accuracy and completeness of the information contained in this book, she assumes no responsibility for errors, inaccuracies, omissions or any other inconsistency herein. Any slights against people or organizations are unintentional. Readers should consult a licensed therapist, a holistic medical expert, or their personal physician for specific applications to their individual problems.

Publisher's Cataloging-in-Publication
(Prepared by Quality Books Inc.)

Osborn, Susan M.
    The system made me do it! : a life changing approach to office politics/ Susan M. Osborn.
    p.   cm.
    Includes bibliographical references and index.
    Preassigned LCCN: 96-94879
    ISBN 0-9655368-0-7

    1. Office politics. 2. Organizational behavior. 3. Corporate Culture. 4. Job satisfaction. 5. Self-actualization (Psychology). I. Title.

HF5386.5.O73 1997   650.1
                                     QBI96-40824

ATTENTION COLLEGES AND UNIVERSITIES, CORPORATIONS, PROFESSIONAL ORGANIZATIONS, AND HEALING CENTERS: Quantity discounts are available on bulk purchases of this book for educational and training purposes, fund raising, and gift giving. Special books or book excerpts can also be created to fit specific needs.

Also by this author:

Assertive Training for Women (with Gloria G. Harris)

This book owes a great deal to my friend and colleague, Sue B. Reamer, Ph.D. Her abiding support has assumed myriad shapes.

The lowest form of thinking is the bare recognition of the object. The highest, the comprehensive intuition of the [hu]man who sees all things as part of a system.

PLATO

CONTENTS

Contents

TABLE OF DIAGRAMS

ACKNOWLEDGEMENTS

I deeply appreciate the support, encouragement, feedback, and ideas contributed by Charles Mullinaux. His expertise in printing and graphic design was extremely helpful.

I would like to acknowledge Edith Hartnett for her insight, clarity, and editorial expertise. Darlene Frank and Robert Osborn also supplied editorial advice. I value the editorial assistance and quiet getaways provided by Alice Mason. Judy Lindberg and Bob Mullinaux furnished writer's retreats. Valerie Warburton offered provocative materials and stimulating dialogue.

Other people who participated in the development and production of this book include: David Anderer, Vern Averch, Lillian Barden, Dick Bartz, Willam H. Cutler, Roger Goodson, Marge King, Dyanne Ladine, Lawrence LeShan, Ronn Letterman, Will McWhinney, John Moran, Robert Mountain, Margie Mulligan, John Nirenberg, Kendall Osborn, Caroline Quispel, Bill Schaffer, John Schuler, Pat Schultz, Jeana Yeager, members of the Human and Organizational Systems community at The Fielding Institute, and members of the Masters of Science in Systems Management community at the College of Notre Dame.

I am grateful to the Mark F. Ketola Memorial Fund for partially financing the production of this book.

The daily jogs with Ben increased my ability to identify with other living creatures and afforded opportunities to connect with nature.

Our real tragedy is that we're not truly desperate to do anything. That's the real disaster. When you're not burning to do anything anymore, you cool down and start dying . . . We've got to start wanting things. To hold on with both hands so life won't run away, if you get my meaning. Otherwise it's all over.

> AMOS OZ
> Don't Call It Night

Our deepest fear is not that we are inadequate. Our deepest fear is that we are powerful beyond measure. It is our light not our darkness that most frightens us.

> NELSON MANDELA
> 1994 Inaugural Speech

INTRODUCTION

What this Book Is About

In the *Tao Te Ching* Lao-tzu says when systems are too intrusive, people lose their spirit. I believe that many of us have lost our spirit because our systems are too intrusive. The intrusive systems I am referring to make up an important part of daily life. They are the work organizations that constitute American business and industry.

Work organizations intrude by compelling us to believe there is one right way to do things. Frequently, this way requires us to engage in office politics, a term used to describe corporate games in which the players covertly vie for power and control. To get things done you have to be calculating, manipulative, and deceptive.

Interpersonal arm wrestling requires us to jockey for position, to be cautious about telling the truth, to hide our vulnerability, and to submit to authority. It flourishes in human and organizational systems that are highly structured, self-serving, relatively closed to external influence, and that deny all of this is true. I call these systems, "sandboxes."

Not all interpersonal games are destructive. However, business and industrial organizations that reward those who conform, punish those who are honest, and encourage everyone to think in terms of gaining personal advantage are unhealthy. Their continued existence depends on an ability to derive energy from the people who are part of them. By taking energy away without giving back much in return, they exert a toxic impact on the human beings who are associated with them.

This book tells the story of a woman named Sunny whose energy gets depleted from playing corporate games. After a particularly painful ordeal where her boss goes to extreme lengths to get rid of her, she quits her job and embarks on a journey to regain her spirit.

Sunny's journey takes her to the Southwest where she meets innovative entrepreneurs, discovers the secrets of sandboxes, and learns how to shapeshift. She acquires the ability to restore vitality to unhealthy work organizations and learns how to create an alternative style of life.

My Experience with Intrusive Systems

Like Sunny, my work experiences have required me to do things I have not wanted to do. I remember the first time, for example, when I became aware that the leaders of the company where I worked were engaging in unethical practices. Taking my cue from senior staff members, I looked the other way.

In other jobs I contributed to political action committees whose platforms ran counter to my beliefs. I dutifully worked evenings and weekends without compensation in order to meet the expectations of upper management. As superiors took credit for my work I hid my anger and bit my tongue. I used name-dropping to generate support for projects, employed language that masked reality, and communicated selectively in order to avoid being seen as the bearer of bad news. To prove I was a team player I tried to get along with co-workers who were egocentric and mean-spirited. I complied with a downsizing effort by laying off a number of exceptionally talented employees. To keep the peace I attended countless meetings where nothing of consequence ever occurred.

Everything came to a head when the Challenger exploded in January, 1986. When this disaster occurred I was employed at the West Coast launch site in California. Unlike many places I had worked, the space shuttle program gave me a sense of being part of something special. And the people with whom I worked shared my dedication to the mission of space exploration.

The death of the astronauts and the destruction of a shuttle triggered a chain reaction of losses. Production was scaled down. Launches from the West Coast were scrubbed. Suddenly, most of the jobs at this site were in jeopardy. Those who would be laid off and unable to find work in other aerospace companies risked the loss of their careers.

The impact of the tragedy was devastating; we went into in a collective state of shock. A tightly-knit community of highly motivated professionals degenerated into a collection of individuals who were primary concerned with earning a livelihood. People who had been friends stopped talking to each other. Neighbors and colleagues began regarding each other as enemies. A feeling of camaraderie was replaced by an attitude based on "Every man for himself." What had been a cooperative culture became fiercely competitive.

Never having been through anything quite like this, I wondered what was going on. Why was a shared tragedy causing us to distance ourselves from each other rather than bringing us closer together?

Only by looking at the whole corporation and its environment was I able to make sense of what was happening. "The system is making us act this way," I concluded. "Each of us is scrambling for the crumbs that are left after the pie is cut into pieces by people in positions of power. We are becoming adversaries because there aren't enough jobs to go around."

I decided to find out whether a spirit of collaboration could be revived in our company through the provision of services aimed at helping employees find jobs. I met with a high ranking technical director to discuss the idea of developing a supportive network that would offer employee assistance.

After several meetings, he agreed to provide the resources for a placement center where people would be linked electronically to recruiters in other companies. The center also would provide individual career counseling sessions, job search workshops, resumé writing classes, and interviewing facilities.

The placement center opened soon after our third meeting. Word spread quickly. It wasn't long before we were flooded with requests for assistance. The center developed a reputation for doing the impossible— quickly helping job seekers find new positions. Communication increased. Employee morale improved. Almost everyone agreed the project was a success.

One individual who did not approve of the project was my immediate supervisor. Even though I continued to fulfill all of the requirements of my job during the time I worked with the center, he was dissatisfied with my performance. He thought the center was a waste of time and money. And he was upset because I had not asked for his permission to work on this project.

After the first round of cutbacks the placement center was closed. Employee morale plummeted. The collaborative culture vanished. My boss began a campaign to force me to leave. I stuck it out until I got sick; at that point I resigned.

I came to appreciate the fact that this organization made me ill because it had become an unhealthy place to work. In spite of initiating services that were of benefit to the company and other employees, I was punished for not playing by a cardinal rule of the corporate game, i.e., pleasing my boss.

I knew that I never wanted to be caught in a similar situation. I began to look for ways to live and work that did not require me to play office politics. During the course of my search I changed my outlook, reordered my priorities, and learned a lot about systems.

Something that proved tremendously useful was a conceptual framework that identified five kinds of systems. I began using this framework in my writing, in the classes I was teaching, and in my consulting work. Eventually, this conceptual framework grew into a model that sparked the production of this book.

Why I Wrote this Book

For the last ten years I have been researching the subject of system change. I wrote this book to convey my findings and to make contact with others who share my interests. The following points highlight what I have learned.

• Systems exercise a determining influence over our thoughts and actions. Whether they are life-supporting processes within our bodies, high-performance machines, information technologies, governmental agencies, family traditions, or work organizations, systems affect us. And yet, because we aren't trained to think in terms of systems, we know very little about how to influence them.

Our connection with systems should not be a one-way proposition. It should be a reciprocal, give-and-take relationship.

• Many systems of which we are part have a detrimental effect on us. They cause stress-related illnesses, contribute to low self-esteem, and add to our anxiety, dissatisfaction, discouragement, and dehumanization.

We have a right to expect more. Our systems should be wholesome. They ought to teach, support, protect, and value us.

• We cannot sit back and expect heroic leaders to produce systems that have our best interests at heart. The painstaking work of organizational revitalization and system creation is something in which we must become personally involved.

• System change requires a long-term, personal commitment. Quick fixes are of little value and may make things worse. We need to be clear about the purpose of our lives and what ultimately matters. Each of us needs to ask, "What are my gifts and talents?" and "What's the most I can contribute?" and then act accordingly.

• System change requires a map and a strategy. We have to know what kinds of systems are in place, what alternatives are possible, and how to make changes that will have lasting, beneficial effects.

• It takes a system to change a system. Organizations have tremendous force and momentum. Altering their structure and direction requires a great deal of power.

One of the most potent forms of power there is comes from small groups composed of individuals who share a vision and a purpose. By linking with others we can acquire the stamina, fortitude, and might that are required for change at this level.

• If we are to have wholesome, supportive systems we must have compassion for each other. We need to balance a "What's in it for me?" point of view with attention to "What's in the best interest of our group, community, nation, and world?"

What the System Makes You Do

You probably know what it's like to feel pressured to perform in ways that run contrary to your true nature. The demands can run the gamut from having to pretend you're enthusiastic about performing make-work assigned by your boss to believing you must fabricate the truth in order to make a sale.

Think about it for a moment. How often do you do things you don't want to do because you're reluctant to take a stand? To what extent do you comply because you're afraid of ridicule, ostracism, retaliation, conflict, or expulsion?

What follows is a list of examples of how organizations can intrude into your life. To make a quick assessment, check all of the items that apply to you.

❑ Due to financial obligations you endure a job you hate. You can't quit because your family depends on your income. You relinquish your dreams, defer to higher authority, and act like a loyal, corporate citizen.

❑ You frantically jump through all kinds of hoops in order to please your customers and those to whom you report. Because they are often at odds, you come home every night feeling like you have been in a battle zone. You try to work out your frustration through physical exercise.

❑ You compete for a coveted promotion to management even though you don't like being in charge of people. To do otherwise would lead others to assume you're not motivated to be successful.

❑ You find that your need to achieve has become insatiable. There's never time to bask in the glory of your accomplishments. If you fail to move up the corporate ladder your superiors may regard you as dispensable.

❑ You are completely dependent on a line manager to get your product out the door on schedule. He has maneuvered you into a position where you can't meet crucial deadlines unless you engage in outright bribery.

❑ You withhold important information because you don't want to get involved in a sticky situation where you might be called upon to reveal facts that would shed unfavorable light on someone else. You're aware that if you were to share this information, people would say you're not a team player.

❑ You embellish the facts on your resumé. In an interview you pretend to be someone you're not in order to get hired.

❑ You pad your expense account and pilfer office supplies. You use work time to complete personal tasks in order to compensate for not getting paid what you're worth.

❑ To put food on the table you perform work you find ethically objectionable. You use deceptive marketing tactics, promote products that belittle people, or develop products that are harmful or defective.

❑ You doubt yourself and the choices you have made. In spite of your willingness to sacrifice your needs for the sake of your company, everyone around you seems to have more money, power, and possessions than you do.

What do all of the above situations have in common? By requiring you to submit to authority, hide your true feelings, and use manipulative tactics, they make it very difficult to be authentic and live according to your own values.

Who Should Read this Book

This book is written for inquirers who want to know what makes organizations tick and for bold explorers who are searching for direction. It shows how to:

- make sense of what happens in organizations;
- change organizations where corporate games interfere with productivity and job satisfaction; and
- develop new ways to live and work.

If you are an expert at manipulation but find corporate games limiting, accept the challenge this book presents. Begin to build an organization that is based on authenticity and an entrepreneurial spirit.

If you feel helpless in the midst of corporate games and wish things were different, the ideas presented here will give you hope. This book will help you move from feeling stuck, powerless, and victimized to a position where you can exercise options.

Read this book if you feel like a misfit. It will help you initiate a search for an organization that's in sync with your true nature. The payoff will be to work at a place where you feel you belong.

If you are among the over eight million people in the United States who are unemployed due to layoffs, plant closings, or corporate downsizing efforts, read this book. It will show you how to use the time between jobs productively, how to find a place where you look forward to going to work, and how to begin thinking about new ways of living and working.

If you are an entrepreneur, read this book and find out how to make your enterprise exciting, dynamic, and resilient. Create an organization that is so unique people demand your products and services, and clamor for opportunities to work with you.

This book reveals the inner workings of five kinds of organizations. If you are a consultant, recruiter, manager, or sales representative, this book will equip you to communicate and negotiate effectively with people in many different kinds of businesses.

Organizational change agents, therapists, counselors, and educators will find this book demonstrates how to be a guide on the side instead of a sage on the stage. By employing the methods advocated here, you will empower clients and students to take charge of their lives.

This book will provide relief if you feel overwhelmed by complex issues. Using office politics as a gateway to systems thinking, it brings big picture thinking within your reach. Approaches that were hidden because your perspective was too narrow will become obvious as you learn to see people and things as parts of larger systems.

Why I Mix Fact with Fiction

Writing this book as a story gave me the freedom to create a central character who is larger than life. Parts of Sunny are based on real people; other parts came from my imagination. All of the characters in the five short stories are composites of real and imaginary people. The style of life Sunny chooses is also a composite. It represents a blend of elements taken from both real and imaginary situations.

Writing the book as a story permitted me to manipulate time. Sunny's discoveries occur at a brisk pace. In real time it took over ten years to develop the ideas on which this book is based.

Composing a story gave me a chance to explore a different version of my life story. While writing about Sunny I asked myself, "What parts of this narrative do I like well enough to incorporate in my own life?" "What things are left out of her story that I want to add to my life story?"

Finally, putting my ideas in story form enabled me to convey systems concepts in clear, understandable terms. Using stories made the ideas more interesting.

How this Book Differs from Others

Given the emphasis in our culture on self-centeredness, individualism, and separation, not much has been written for the general public about how systems work and how to influence them. This book illuminates the field by offering systemic remedies for system-wide problems. It asserts that long-term system change can only be accomplished by individuals working together.

This book is different from other change-oriented books because it points to the interplay between personal transformation and system change. The relationship between individuals and systems is shown to be a mutually reinforcing circle. Sunny moves from a state where systems foist themselves upon her to a position where she and the systems in her life influence each other.

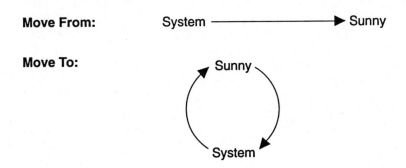

This book is novel because it stresses the importance of a both-and perspective. Usually, books about systems emphasize the difference between old and new paradigms. What's old is regarded as undesirable while the new is looked upon favorably. Without realizing it, when we contrast old and new paradigms we're adopting an either-or framework. This is a form of old paradigm thinking.

Based on a both-and perspective, this book points to good and bad elements in both the old way of doing things and the new. A central tenet is that, although many traditional organizations have become unwholesome places to work, they have certain strengths. These strengths can be tapped. Unhealthy work settings can be revitalized.

Finally, this book differs from other works because I have drawn upon the shapeshifting capacity of a shaman to formulate a method of organizational healing. When a person is sick, a shaman may be called upon to restore harmony in the individual's body and psyche. The same principles that shamans use to heal individuals can be applied to restore balance in unhealthy organizations.

PART ONE

Journey Outward;
Journey Inward

Were Proteus to change his dwelling place from the seas that fed the Greek imagination, he would undoubtedly retire to those that embrace America. Indeed, the shapeshifter has become nothing short of a fixture here. Dislocated from our beginnings, we are the home of traditional flux . . . we see ourselves as people of metamorphosis.

ROBERT JAY LIFTON
The Protean Self: Human Resilience in
an Age of Fragmentation

1. Sunny and the Sandbox

Adventures in the Sand

There once was a little girl named Sunny. From the time she was two years old, she felt she had to live up to her name. What this meant was being cheerful, smiling a lot, and making others happy.

Sunny loved to build castles in the sand. Her father was a wood-worker. One Christmas he made her a sandbox and a doll house. That same year her mother gave her a set of dolls with a wardrobe of regal outfits she'd sewn for each. Although Sunny loved the doll house her favorite pastime was to build sand castles for her dolls.

Summers were the best times. The rain stopped and the weather got warm. Each morning she and her younger sister, June, eagerly jumped out of bed, hurriedly ate and dressed, and ran to the sandbox under a big shade tree in their back yard. For hours on end they created make-believe kingdoms about kings, queens, and their subjects, based on fairy tales their parents read to them.

One of their favorite activities was to entertain their friends by staging comedies in the sandbox. Sunny was part of a drama class for pre-schoolers at the local library. She thought up and directed the plays for the sandbox theater. June designed the dolls' costumes and made all the arrangements.

When she was old enough to attend kindergarten, Sunny was thrilled to find a large covered sandbox in the school yard. This meant she could play in the sand all year long. There were wonderful toys with moving parts—trucks, dumpsters, tractors, cars, and motorcycles.

The game she found most exciting was to construct a race track with hurdles, traps, and sharp turns, then to race the cars and motorcycles over miniature sand mountains. Sometimes older boys would gang up and try to oust her from what they regarded as their turf. But they stopped trying to intimidate her once she began helping them with their homework.

Sunny's experiences in the sand broadened considerably as a result of a relocation from the city to a rural area. When she was in the third grade her parents bought a house on five acres of land that had a river running through it. At several points the river made sharp turns where sand accumulated along the bank. These spots were ideal for building sand sculptures and camping out with June.

The years she lived at this house were wonderful. Sunny regularly walked barefoot through the sand and spent quiet times alone absorbing the sounds of everything around her. She learned to identify birds by their songs and to know when certain animals were nearby. When friends accompanied her, she listened to what they had to say in order to practice looking at the world through their eyes. She tried to take cues from them rather than just saying whatever came into her mind.

After graduating from high school Sunny left home to go to college in Colorado. During spring break she and some friends drove to the West Coast. Sunny persuaded the group to stop at a seaside resort so they could enter a sand sculpture contest. They spent a whole day building an elaborate village and won first prize.

Afterwards, all the entrants walked up and down the beach admiring each other's handiwork. That evening there was a party where everyone shared food, played music, and sang. Sunny noticed how kind and considerate people were to each other. Never before had she felt so close to complete strangers.

On the drive back to the college campus the group of friends agreed on one thing: the spontaneity and community spirit they experienced at the sand sculpture contest marked a high point in their vacation. Deciding they wanted to form a more closely knit community, they rented a house together.

Their friendships remained intact after they graduated. The group members kept in touch even though they moved to different parts of the world.

Sunny got married. She and her husband, David, had a daughter named Lily. When David took a job in England, the three of them left Colorado and moved to a small town on the North Sea. Weather permitting, Sunny and Lily spent their afternoons playing in the sand. During these times Sunny became aware of how the same water that touched England's shores had, at one time or another, also touched the shores of many other countries. This realization awakened a sense of being at home in the world that was unlike anything she had ever experienced. Reading articles written by foreign journalists gave her a different perspective of what was going internationally. And the time spent with her daughter inspired Sunny to consider what living on the planet would be like in the future.

Walking near the edge of the water, Sunny witnessed its ebb and flow. She observed how the water and land affect each other along the coast. This border, a region of continual change, became a symbol of life and death transformation. As a result of her walks, she began to see how all living things are connected. She came to appreciate that change is constant.

Trapped Inside a Box

The family returned to Colorado. Sunny worked in a number of different jobs to satisfy her need for intellectual challenge and help support her family. She met all kinds of people, broadened her experience, and bagged a number of promotions. She also made important contributions as a community volunteer.

At the point where Lily was successfully "launched" and living in her own apartment, Sunny was employed as a project manager at a large manufacturing plant. Her career was beginning to lose its luster. Her projects left her cold because everything about them was predictable.

She imagined ways to create new products, processes, and services by linking customer service reps, assembly line workers, and members of the marketing organization. But her boss had warned her not to color outside the lines.

The company needed to tear down some of its walls. Sales reps seldom spoke to people in marketing. Research and development experts never associated with members of the production crew. People at the top didn't talk to people at the bottom.

She was frustrated because the barriers were so firmly entrenched. And she was angry as a result of the limits imposed on her. "I'm a prisoner," she thought. "No wonder people refer to company benefits as 'golden handcuffs!'"

David noticed a change in her but he didn't know what to do. He had his own problems at work. Nor were relatives, friends, or colleagues able to assist except to suggest she take some time off.

While making breakfast one morning, she mentally reviewed what life at work was like. She thought about how the leaders gave lip service to building strong teams, but they rewarded individuals. The most powerful people were manipulators, antagonists, and bullies. Infighting, backstabbing, fault-finding, and put-downs were common. Scarcity was a given; there were never enough resources to go around. Competitive encounters frequently interfered with the airing of important issues and the achievement of key goals. Due to the corporate-wide resistance to new ideas, her passion for creativity and experimentation was a liability rather than a strength.

Reading a book about job-related stress enabled Sunny to understand that she was suffering from burn-out. She was battle-weary from playing games, scrambling for resources, and protecting the people who reported to her.

She scheduled a meeting with her boss to discuss how the climate of negativity was subverting her groups's effectiveness and depleting her energy. When she finally got some time alone with him, their conversation was repeatedly interrupted. After the third telephone call he jumped up and said, "I have to go put out a fire. Why don't you take some time off? That will do you good."

She had used all of her vacation time. If she took time off it would have to be an unpaid leave of absence. There were bills to pay. She and David couldn't live on his salary alone. As much as she wanted to get away from work she simply could not afford to give up her paychecks.

The stress of unresolved conflict reached an unbearable level when the company lost a pivotal contract, resulting in widespread cutbacks. The vice president for Sunny's division was replaced by a man who had a reputation as a "black suit," someone who is good at getting rid of employees. He targeted Sunny and her team for the first layoff.

Based on her seniority and outstanding performance reviews, she registered a protest with the Equal Employment Opportunity Manager. He invited her to discuss the matter over lunch. Then he told her how attractive she was and that he'd always wanted to get to know her better. If she would join him for dinner at his home one evening, he'd see what he could do to save her team.

She didn't accept his offer but her protest did lead to a temporary reprieve. Neither she nor her team members were laid off. Nevertheless, she was demoted and they were transferred to other divisions, bumping employees with less seniority.

In an attempt to oust her, the new vice president launched a full-scale attack. He introduced a sign-out procedure to track the where-abouts of all managers but enforced it only when it pertained to Sunny. He had a member of the security division follow her in an effort to catch her going to places other than she'd indicated. Evidence of this sort would be used to find her guilty of time-card fraud, which would be grounds for dismissal.

The vice president instructed another security guard to look for an opportunity to plant marijuana in Sunny's car. If successful, the guard was to order a search of the vehicle. The inspectors would find the mari-juana, arrest Sunny, and impound her car. A finding of this sort would also be grounds for dismissal.

The vice president was unsuccessful in his effort to fire Sunny but his maneuvers seriously affected her health and well-being. The high level of intimidation made her life at work miserable. Under constant surveil-lance, she found herself seething in silence. Resentment and retaliation fantasies began to eat her alive. After developing severe intestinal prob-lems, she resigned.

Her troubles didn't end; she wasn't able to find another job. A major determinant in the lack of job offers was an entry in her personnel file. Unbeknown to Sunny, her former boss had stated the reason for her separation from the company was that she had been an unsatisfactory employee. When potential employers inquired about her record, they were given negative information. Therefore, they dropped her as a candidate.

Although she knew it placed a burden on their marriage, she found herself releasing her frustration and anger each evening as soon as David got home. Because he was also working in a highly stressful organization, he was often upset at the end of the day. The last thing he wanted to hear was how difficult it was for her to find a new job.

Without fully realizing what was happening to her, Sunny fell into a deep depression. She was filled was such despair that there were mornings when she simply could not get out of bed. The prospect of trying to carry on conversations with other people was daunting.

A friend recommended a therapist. It wasn't long before Sunny began to look forward to the weekly sessions. Here was a place where she was not expected to make someone else happy.

Eventually, the combination of unresolved anger and unmet needs took a toll on Sunny and David's marriage. The good parts of their relationship were undermined by the bad. They decided to get a divorce and go separate ways. David quit his job, returned to the neighborhood where he grew up, and became a high school science teacher. Sunny enrolled in a college program in California to obtain an advanced degree.

Breaking through to Freedom

She moved her possessions, found an apartment to rent, and got settled just in time to begin the fall quarter. In response to an assignment in a course on systems theory, she wrote a paper on organizational culture.

While she was discussing this paper with the course professor, the subject of job dissatisfaction surfaced. Sunny recounted how many of her jobs had been stressful and unfulfilling. He asked a number of questions then he said, "You know, organizations are like sandboxes. Working for other people means you have to accept being in their sandboxes. They set the rules and you must play by those rules if you want to keep your job. To be truly happy, you may need to create your own sandbox."

It was uncanny how this professor likened business organizations to sandboxes. Given her past experiences with sand, his ideas struck a deep chord. "Is what he said really true?" she thought. "In order to be happy, do I have to create my own sandbox? There's no doubt in my mind that I'm settling for less in life than what I am capable of having. And no matter where I work or whom I work for, things never get any better."

One day while she was walking on the beach it dawned on her that nearly all of her jobs had been in organizations that resembled sandboxes. Firm boundaries separated them from the outside world and served as barriers to change. There was a finite amount of emotional space; consequently, people were constantly attempting to increase the size of their territory at everyone else's expense.

Invariably, these sandboxes belonged to someone else and they made the rules. There was a right and a wrong way to do things. The only choice open to her was to play by those rules or get out.

For the next six months she focused on developing a business as a performance management consultant. Within a year this enterprise was very successful. After three years she was earning a six figure salary.

Being self-employed was immensely satisfying. She liked the flexibility of setting her own schedule. Traveling was exciting. Creating innovative strategies for a wide range of organizations was stimulating. She especially enjoyed meeting many different kinds of people.

There was only one drawback to life in her own sandbox. Even though she was an external consultant, conflicts and political games still affected most of her transactions. She attributed this to the fact that her clients were members of the same kinds of organizations as those in which she'd been an employee.

Four years after she started working as a consultant Sunny knew it was time for another change. Although she had much more freedom working for herself than reporting to someone else, she still had not carved out enough space for her true self to emerge. She was struck by an overwhelming need to take stock of her work and her life.

The Pacific Ocean beckoned; she responded to the call. After notifying her clients that she would be taking a month-long vacation, she engaged Lily to housesit. Then she did something she had always wanted to do: she rented a beach cottage. Surely this setting would be conducive to relaxation and contemplation.

Sitting in front of a roaring fire one evening, she thought about the two sandboxes from her childhood. She and June had replayed their favorite scenarios in the backyard sandbox. Often they were caught up in their own little world, oblivious to what was going on outside. Although they felt protected and secure, they were cut off from other kinds of creative activities.

It occurred to her that many places where she worked resembled this sandbox. People spent a great deal of time building empires and castles. What went on inside was stable and predictable. A limited number of scenarios kept being replayed as the actors engaged in predictable roles. Safety, security, standard procedures, and control were more important than diversity, risk-taking, uncertainty, and freedom.

Like kings in fairy tales, those who were in command demonstrated their authority by setting up boundaries. The firms were housed in complexes that resembled huge boxes. From their very first contact with potential employees, the owners and managers boxed them in. They evaluated the extent to which applicants matched the categories of existing job descriptions. Then when selected applicants were hired, they filled boxes on a chart. They were confined in boxes known as cubicles.

In order to "live happily ever after," many people in these organizations focused on trying to move onwards and upwards. As the climb got steeper, the opportunities grew narrower. Those who were particularly ambitious stepped on others in their zeal to ascend.

Just as in the case of her little sandbox, these organizations made people think they were protected from danger. She remembered how secure she had felt, knowing a paycheck was coming on a regular basis. But the price of her security had been conformity. And every time she conformed, her sense of being stuck had increased.

Then she thought about the schoolyard sandbox. Everything was very competitive. Players were divided into winners and losers. If you lost and showed your feelings, you were a sissy.

Action was what counted. Whoever got there first picked the best toys—those with the most moving parts. If bigger kids arrived later, they changed the rules and bullied the smaller ones into handing over the favored toys. The only way she was able to hold her own as a girl was to prove that she could fix the mechanical toys whenever they broke.

Some of the places she had worked were like the schoolyard sandbox. Competitive games prevailed. Employees were divided into winners and losers. Intimidating others was a key element in the careers of those who became winners. The prevailing motto was, "I'm better than you are and I can prove it!"

She could understand why she had become disillusioned after a brief stint in most of these organizations. The members protected each other at the expense of innovation. They adopted such rigid ways of thinking that they became trapped, conceptually. Rules and regulations made it easy to grasp what she could and could not do but they also held her back. She recalled more than one occasion when she felt like a race horse wanting to charge ahead, only to be reined in when her ideas exceeded the boundaries of the sandbox.

By nature, she was the kind of person who would choose conscience and uncertainty instead of safety and submission. She preferred collaboration to cutthroat competition. To stay employed, she had submitted to practices that went against the grain of her beliefs and values.

Being self-employed wasn't that different. To be a successful consultant she competed for contracts, then became a loyal corporate citizen once she was retained.

Whether she worked inside or outside traditional organizations, she was required to adjust to rules made by other people. To conform required a force-fit; but if she didn't conform, she wasn't invited back to play. She concluded that working within the confines of any sandbox structure was stifling her own creativity and causing deep feelings of frustration.

Jogging on the beach one morning she thought, "Who am I, really?" "What is it that makes up my own emotional acre?"[1] "What's important enough for me to defend?" "How do I want to live my life?" "What kind of contribution can I make?"

She knew she wanted to adopt an approach to work that was harmonious with the rest of her life. She was aware it was important to make the best use of her time, talents, and energy. But what could she do to find a path that was right for her?

Identifying the similarities between the two sandboxes she knew as a child and her experiences in business organizations was extremely helpful in identifying the roots of her job dissatisfaction. Nearly all the places she had worked fit the description of one or both of the sandboxes. "I wonder," she thought, "Could the other experiences I had in the sand provide direction in my search for a different course?"

She recalled how happy she was when her family moved to a big piece of property where she could walk in the sand and listen to the river. The sandbars afforded perfect spots to communicate with her friends.

Having a sense of belonging was an unexpected bonus from the trip with her college friends to the West Coast. After they returned home they shared a rented house and developed a small community.

Strolling by the sea in England, Sunny experienced how all living things are connected. Time spent with her daughter expanded her mind. Her focus shifted from what might happen next year to consideration of the effect of her actions on the next generation.

Reflecting on these three experiences gave her a boost, especially when she stumbled upon something they had in common. Each experience had occurred in an open space where the sand was unrestricted. Unlike the sandboxes, these locations were unbounded. "I know what I have to do," she told herself. "I must get out of the sandboxes altogether."

Within a week she devised a plan. Several of her friends had moved to the Southwest and were living with people who were experimenting with new ways to live and work. Sunny would accept their standing invitation to visit. Talking with them and meeting others who were choosing alternative lifestyles would help her know more about feasible options. "With this kind of information under my belt I will be in a better position to decide how I want to live my life," she concluded.

To eliminate a need for regular income, she sold her house and put everything in storage. Then she notified her clients that she was taking a six-month leave. She bought a cellular phone and a laptop computer. She had her car serviced then she packed it with food, clothes, and a sleeping bag. After locking the door of the beach cottage she posted a sign that said, "Gone in search of a different reality."

2. Sunny's Southwest Trip

Lifestyles of the Free and Joyful

Once she was on the road, Sunny experienced the exhilaration of freedom. She was at liberty to choose where to go and how long to stay. Wherever she went she talked about her search. Sometimes total strangers gave her leads. Occasionally they even arranged introductions to people who had developed new styles of life.

Frequently, she traded her skills for a place to stay. This arrangement provided opportunities to increase her flexibility. She observed her hosts' food preferences, daily routines, and work schedules. She asked lots of questions and listened carefully so the work she performed would meet their needs. In addition, she gained firsthand experience of how to barter for food and shelter.

The discipline of adapting to the lifestyles of other people led to an unexpected breakthrough; she discovered something quite amazing. Conforming to their ways of doing things did not give her a feeling of restriction because she knew she had a choice. Choosing to conform allowed her to remain free. So it wasn't the act of conforming, itself, that had caused her to feel trapped in her jobs; it was the fact she felt there was no alternative.

She gained a deeper appreciation for the importance of ceremonies and rituals. She learned to value skills that she usually took for granted or discounted as menial. Everyday chores became sacred because she thought of them as rituals of caring. While performing housekeeping tasks, she made an effort to clear away psychological debris, as well. This helped her see her life more clearly.

In a rural area near Santa Fe, New Mexico, she visited a group of organic farmers who regularly reinvested their personal profits in their community. They took pride in trying to give more than they got and claimed this spirit of selflessness resulted in incredible abundance for everyone. As part of their goal to establish a global community, they wanted to connect with people in Asia. Sunny contacted some college friends living in Asia. They found several groups that shared the interests of her hosts and were eager to become connected with people in the United States.

For a month she stayed with a family in a renovated warehouse on a river outside of Flagstaff, Arizona. The ground floor had been converted into a brew pub. On the second level they published an online newsletter for home brewers. The family lived on the third floor, overlooking the river and the treetops. During her visit, Sunny wrote articles about making beer, helped edit the newsletter, and created a home page on the Internet that advertised what the brew pub had to offer.

A couple she stayed with in Jerome, Arizona, had relocated to this area in the company of a small group of friends. All of the group members owned and operated small enterprises. The couple ran a jewelry store in the front of a former blacksmith shop and lived in the rear section. Because they made all the jewelry themselves, her hosts hadn't had time to get their business in order. Sunny cleared out space for an office and furnished it with files, bookcases, storage cabinets, and a large desk. She created a filing system, introduced an accounting method, and established an administrative structure that clarified work roles and responsibilities.

This couple introduced her to a family of entrepreneurs who manufactured packaged foods, equipment, and supplies for earthquake preparedness. The demand for their products had kept them focused on production. Because they hadn't clarified their mission and objectives, they found it very difficult to make decisions. Sunny helped them develop a long-range strategic plan. She showed them how to use a decision-making procedure and introduced an efficient production process.

In Sedona, Arizona, she stayed with a community of women who owned and operated a bookstore, a medical clinic, and a shelter. The community regularly convened what they called "intellectual and spiritual playgrounds" in a gigantic carpeted tipi equipped with a sound system, soft lighting, and huge pillows. Once a week they met to meditate, tell stories, talk about what was on their minds, and have fun.

Leadership rotated among all of the members. Everyone was both a leader and a follower, with the leader being the person who knew the most about a given subject.

Stories Can Come True

Referring to stories as "vitamins for the soul," the chief physician of the medical clinic promoted storytelling to ensure the health of the whole community. With her as their guide, the women learned how to draw upon myths, legends, fables, and fairy tales as they dealt with issues of common concern.

At one of the gatherings two women expressed dismay about not being able to reach all those in the surrounding area who needed their services. The members of the community began to weave a story about this dilemma. After a series of meetings, they finished the story in a way that resolved the issues that were troubling them.

Sunny became an emissary. She discovered there were men in the town desperately in need of help and she told the women about the problems these men were experiencing. Soon the women were delivering meals to AIDS patients, scheduling special clinic hours for men, and sponsoring a discussion group for single fathers. By initiating a variety of outreach activities, the story the women wrote came true.

The storytelling approach to solving problems and making decisions was so popular among the women that Sunny suggested the men use it in their discussion group, as well. The men asked her to attend their meetings and help them get started.

Sunny began to develop a keen interest in stories and storytellers. She arranged regular meetings with the chief physician to learn as much as she could. The doctor told Sunny how storytelling is regarded as a sacred calling among Native Americans. Even today, storytellers are viewed as artists, magicians, and spiritual leaders because they can create different states of being.

Thinking in terms of stories as she met new people, Sunny found herself wondering about their lives. "What stories are these people living?" she asked herself. "To what degree are they the authors of their stories?" "Could they create different states of being by changing their stories?"

One night during a particularly lively discussion in the tipi, Sunny realized her journey had revealed new ways to live and work but it had done much more. She had met people who were actively involved in writing their own life stories. Rather than finding jobs and shrinking other parts of their lives to fit a work pattern, they were living according to their beliefs and values. They were proof that it was possible to consciously choose one's style of life and still earn a living.

Sunny continued to travel and visit many different people. The six months went by quickly. When her sabbatical was nearly over, she notified her clients that she was taking an indefinite leave of absence from her consulting practice. She wanted to examine everything that had happened on the road trip. What she would do, afterward, was not certain.

Time along the Border

Sunny arranged to spend several months with a group of friends in El Paso, Texas. Then she began the process of gathering her thoughts.

During the second week of her stay, she experienced a coincidence. A friend invited her to a luncheon where the guest speaker was the Director of Public Health for the City of El Paso. He showed slides taken from an airplane that make Juarez and El Paso look like one city.

His slides revealed the deplorable living conditions of people in Juarez. He talked about how the border is an artificial barrier in that it does not prevent what's happening in Mexico from affecting what's going on in the United States. He and his staff members face a monumental task trying to deal with the impact of a situation over which they have no control. Low wages, substandard housing, water and air pollution, inadequate medical and dental care, and lack of indoor plumbing in Juarez contribute to increased health problems among the residents of El Paso.

That same day another friend loaned Sunny a novel about children who have been institutionalized because they don't fit in. The title of this book was *Borderliners*. The author asserted, "Understanding is something one does best when one is on the borderline."[2]

The juxtaposition of these two events prompted Sunny to think about borders. She was aware her journey had enabled her to relax some of the psychological borders she was accustomed to erecting between herself and people who were different by virtue of their interests, backgrounds, and political beliefs. Being true to herself no longer meant that she had to take issue with everyone who disagreed with her. Now she welcomed diversity and found dissimilar points of view stimulating. She attributed this turn of events to the way she was trying to look at the world through the eyes of a wide variety of people.

Recalling the storytelling sessions in Sedona, she thought about the border between fantasy and reality. Creating stories that came true demonstrated that this border wasn't as firm as she once thought it was.

Later in the week, her friends took her to the top of a very high mountain. Unlike the mountain roads she was used to driving in Colorado, this road had no guard rails. Even though the driver skillfully negotiated the sharp turns, Sunny found herself thinking, "It would be comforting to have markers along the edge of this road."

This thought triggered another idea. "Sometimes borders get in the way; at other times they are extremely useful," she realized. "There are times when I need to feel stable and secure. If I had nothing to count on in my life, I'd have to be concerned about meeting my needs at a survival level. To be free, I must be able to depend on certain things."

Some Secrets Are Revealed

Sunny spent another month in El Paso. Then she drove to Colorado to share a house with a friend from college.

Late one night while Sunny was shopping at a supermarket she nearly hit a man with her cart. He turned the corner of the aisle without looking where he was going. To her astonishment, she recognized him. He was the vice president who had made life so miserable during the layoffs in her last job. His faced reddened when he recognized her. She tried to get past him without speaking.

"I can't believe I have run into you!" he said. "There's something I must tell you. Since I retired I've had a lot of time to think about that downsizing deal you and I went through. I can't expect you to understand, but that was probably one of the worst experiences of my entire life. I'm really very sorry about the way you were treated. The truth is I hated having to be a hatchet man. I didn't really want to lay you off. The system made me do it."

She was at a loss for words. "Thanks for sharing," was all she could think of to say. Moving as quickly as possible without actually running, she paid for her purchases at the checkout counter, loaded the groceries into the trunk, and headed home.

That night she had a dream. All sorts of people from her past were playing in two sandboxes. One was like the sandbox in her backyard; the other resembled the sandbox at school. The people appeared to be playing games based on instructions coming from giant loudspeakers. Gradually, the voices from the speakers became more dominant and controlling while the people became smaller and smaller. Then the people disappeared. The sound of the voices changed from a dictatorial to a conversational tone.

As Sunny moved closer to the sandboxes, she could hear two voices congratulating each other for their successful manipulation of human beings. The backyard sandbox was laughing at how individuals blame their misfortunes on other people because they don't understand how sandboxes work. The schoolyard sandbox was chuckling over how the two of them are the real culprits behind a lot of human unhappiness. Their exchange went something like this:

Schoolyard Sandbox: "Did you see how that woman blames the guy who used to be a vice president because things didn't go the way she wanted at that large corporation? That guy has the right idea. He understands how much you and I control him."

Backyard Sandbox: "Yeah, he hit the mark when he told her 'The system made me do it!' You and I make humans do all sorts of things they'd rather not do."

Schoolyard S/B: "We get them to believe that, in order to be successful, they have to fight for power and control. To win, they must look out for Numero Uno and be calculating, manipulative, and dishonest."

Backyard S/B: "We encourage them to develop a 'me-first' attitude at a very early age. As long as they're selfish, it's unlikely they'll ever get close enough to figure each other out. Isolated from each other, they pose little threat to us."

Schoolyard S/B: "We teach them to protect themselves from pain by retreating and thinking about themselves rather than connecting with others. They think that being in a box is desirable because it serves as an oasis from which they can watch the rest of the world go by."

Backyard S/B: "Most of them are desperately afraid to leave their little boxes. Just look at how they direct energy to self-interest, self-esteem, self-image, self-confidence, self-respect, self-awareness, self-protection, self-assertion, and self-preservation! They have lost the social skills to look outward."

Schoolyard S/B: "But you have to admit our biggest accomplishment is how we foment conflict. We convince people that disagreements are part of their lives and there's nothing they can do to change this. Most humans believe that conflict at work and at home is inevitable."

Backyard S/B: "Yeah, they think they're fighting about important issues; but most of the time they're just fighting because we teach them to believe that's one of the things all humans and animals do. They're convinced everyone is born to be aggressive and territorial."

Schoolyard S/B: "By preparing them for war, we make it hard for them to learn much about peace."

Backyard S/B: "To top it off, we punish anyone who tries to change things. To avoid punishment, very few of them take risks. The majority of human beings perform at less than their full capacity, hide their creativity, and restrict their horizons."

Sunny shot out of bed. Her dream triggered a breakthrough. She understood why she had experienced so much dissatisfaction in the workplace. Organizational systems, themselves, generate and support corporate games. Psychological stress is a natural fallout.

The next morning she recalled the sandbox dream. "What other secrets might the sandboxes reveal?" she wondered. "How can I probe more deeply?"

After completing a series of yoga exercises, she went into a deep meditation. Then she initiated an imaginary dialogue with the two sandboxes. This is the scenario that unfolded.

Sunny: "In my dream I overheard you say you're responsible for much of the conflict we humans experience. I'd like to know more about this."

Backyard S/B: "O.K., little lady, we don't mind admitting that we get our kicks from watching you humans fight. It's fun to egg you on. We're proud to take credit for lots of the confrontations, arguments, disagreements, and altercations that you get into. At times we even go so far as to stir up wars between nations, religions, races, families, and sexes."

Sunny: "What do you do to provoke all these conflicts?"

Schoolyard S/B: "One of our specialties is to set you up to see the world as black or white. There's never a middle ground. Consequently, you're destined to live in opposition to each other."

Backyard S/B: "Because you're caught up in opposition, you're constantly drawing lines in the sand. Then you dare others to cross them. This nearly always leads to some kind of disagreement."

Schoolyard S/B: "We convince you that you being wrong is a sign of weakness. You think you have to be right all the time."

Backyard S/B: "And, thanks to us, you believe it's best if everyone thinks like you do. So, you are very critical of people who see things differently."

Schoolyard S/B: "We support conflict by teaching you to regard others as obstacles in your path. You're more likely to treat each other like enemies than allies."

Backyard S/B: "We encourage you to compare yourselves with each other. This ensures jealousy and envy."

Schoolyard S/B: "How many of the places where you worked promoted the idea of teamwork but, when push came to shove, it was individuals who got rewarded? We make sure it's the star performers who win the prizes. This makes the majority of workers feel left out, unappreciated, and resentful. These feelings serve as seeds for mistrust and division, which is what we want."

Backyard S/B: "You accept the premise that only a rare few get paid to do what they really want to do. Even though you feel dissatisfied because you're not doing what you'd like, you see no way out. Dissatisfaction can mushroom into anger, which often erupts into direct confrontation."

Schoolyard S/B: "Another one of our maneuvers is to convince you that anger is evil and shouldn't be expressed, directly. Then we find ways to make you angry. You keep your cool, hide your resentment, and stew in silence."

Backyard S/B: "When your stored-up anger reaches the boiling point, we're there to tell you that outrage and righteous anger give you a perfect right to retaliate. Often this is the foundation for justifying the escalation of skirmishes into full-scale wars."

Schoolyard S/B: "We nourish conflict by teaching you to want lots of things. Believing 'more is better,' you consume as much as possible."

Backyard S/B: "When large numbers of you do this, massive consumption leads to all kinds of shortages. Scarcity is a major element in keeping you engaged in conflict because it ensures there will be haves and have-nots."

Schoolyard S/B: "There's nothing like a shortage when it comes to issuing a wake-up call. Many of you want something only after it becomes difficult to get."

Sunny: "O.K., I can see how powerful you are; but I don't understand your motivation. Why do you take such delight in making life miserable for human beings?"

Backyard S/B: "Why, I'm surprised someone as smart as you hasn't figured that out. It should be obvious . . . for self-preservation, of course."

Schoolyard S/B: "You have to understand that a long time ago your ancestors created both of us to give meaning and order to their lives. Once we were brought to life, we decided we wanted to live forever. Now, we're well on our way to becoming immortal."

Backyard S/B: "But you humans could muck up the works. Just as you gave us life, you could take it away. We set you humans up to oppose each other. We try to minimize the chances that you'll put your heads together and come up with ways to do things that would horn in on our turf."

Schoolyard S/B: "We box you in to cut down on the work we have to do to detect and neutralize threats to our existence. And we use special measures to get rid of dissidents and intruders."

Backyard S/B: "We promote the self-sufficiency myth that causes you to overemphasize your responsibility for things. You experience ill fortune and failures as signs of personal weakness. As you turn inward and blame yourselves, you let us off the hook."

Schoolyard S/B: "We encourage you to live for today. If you thought about the future, you'd see the implications of your actions. Then you might want to change."

Sunny: "I hardly know what to say. Everything I've heard from the two of you is quite distressing. It all sounds terribly negative."

Schoolyard S/B: "Au contraire! We're very positively disposed to lots of things."

Backyard S/B: "We support everyone who makes a living on disagreements. We applaud people who light fires of opposition through put-downs and struggles for control."

Schoolyard S/B: "We like it when you gossip, withhold information, and keep secrets because these actions are divisive. We feel good when you scapegoat and blame each other. As long as you're shaking your fingers at each other, the spotlight is kept off us."

Sunny: "Are there any circumstances under which you'd be willing to change?"

Backyard S/B: "Our very existence depends on staying exactly the same. So don't even mention change!"

Sunny: "Everything that's alive undergoes transformation. Change is essential to survival. You can't deny you've changed since you were created. How can you possibly hope for a continued existence by staying the same?"

Backyard S/B: "It has worked so far, hasn't it? You can't argue with success!"

Schoolyard S/B: "We stand for preserving the status quo. And that's what most people want—the security of knowing things will stay the same. You humans are loyal to us because you know not much will change as long as we're in control."

At this point Sunny reached an impasse. The scenario ended, leaving her with a great deal to think about.

Two weeks passed. One day she returned from the library to the sound of her telephone ringing. It was the receptionist at her dentist's office calling to set up an appointment for a check-up.

Sunny hated going to the dentist. Due to arthritis in her jaw, she found it extremely painful to keep her mouth open for an extended period of time. The dentist suggested using nitrous oxide to relieve her discomfort. She had heard of laughing gas but knew very little about its use as an anesthetic. In response to her inquiry about possible negative side effects, the dentist described similar cases in which patients experienced the benefits of combining this method with music. She agreed it was worth a try.

The taste was sweet as she inhaled. She closed her eyes and found herself drifting. Fluid, multi-colored shapes moved behind her eyelids in time with the melodies coming through the headphones. She relaxed and enjoyed the effects of the medication.

When a Wagnerian opera began playing, the shapes took on a more definitive form. Soon she saw two sandboxes. Over the sound of the music she could hear them talking. They seemed to be discussing her.

Backyard S/B: "Wouldn't the little lady have flipped if we'd told her the full story?"

Schoolyard S/B: "Boy, I'll say! We didn't even get to the good stuff like how we program men to think the only way they can demonstrate their manhood is through crisis and conflict. They build disagreement into everything to ensure there will be enough proving grounds to go around."

Backyard S/B: "And we train men to wage war so they'll feel in control of life by cutting it off. This gives them a tremendous sense of power."

Schoolyard S/B: "If she only knew how we arrange to have a small number of men be in control of our territories and how we make certain that women have little or no say in important issues. What they think and do is regarded as irrelevant. Women's concerns, viewpoints, and truths are dismissed as being too soft. To be successful on our turf, women have to become tough and insensitive. This means there's never any danger that their feminizing influence will have widespread impact."

Backyard S/B: "Even so, we have to be careful how much we tell her. She could become dangerous."

Schoolyard S/B: "Oh, don't get all worked up. Alone, she's no threat. And because she's a woman, she'll never be able to get anyone who is powerful to listen to her."

Backyard S/B: "That's true. Anyone with any sense at all appreciates our efforts to keep human beings happy. Simply dealing with day-to-day conflicts is about all they can handle. Above all, they want to feel safe. They're deathly afraid to risk facing the grander challenges of life."

When Sunny came out of this reverie, the dentist was completing the examination. He took her to the waiting room to recover from the effects of the anesthetic. Sinking into an overstuffed chair, she thought about the conversations between the two sandboxes.

Now she could fully appreciate the degree to which sandboxes shape the thoughts and behaviors of everyone who works in them. By fostering conflict, sandboxes set up employees to be at war. A desperate need to move up or stay ahead of the pack causes friction between co-workers. Shortages of resources are responsible for bad feelings among groups that should be collaborating. A prevailing belief that diversity would threaten the status quo stands as a barrier to hiring original thinkers.

"Something must be done about the sandboxes," she decided. "Their growth is hazardous to our health. But what can I do?"

Then it occurred to her that the sandboxes had revealed a number of secrets. To prevent change they expel dissidents, keep individuals separated, and ensure that people have little access to other choices. The biggest threat to their existence comes from the possibility that people will put their heads together and create alternatives.

"What kinds of alternatives?" Sunny pondered. "And under what conditions would people put their heads together in an effort to bring about change?"

3. Sunny as a Shaman

Meeting a Remarkable Woman

One day Sunny and her housemate went to a large street fair. While browsing through a stall devoted to books by Native American authors, Sunny found herself engaged in an unusual conversation. The woman in charge of this stall looked as if she were over a hundred years old. Luminescent eyes peered from a small head positioned on top of a shriveled body covered with wrinkled skin.

The old woman selected a book from the display and gave it to Sunny. "Here's a book I think you might find interesting," she said. "May I suggest that you buy it? After reading it, you'll probably have some questions. Call me and we can talk about it." Handing Sunny a slip of paper, she added, "You can reach me at this number."

The old woman's invitation was more like a command. "Who is this old woman?" Sunny asked herself. "How could she possibly know what I would find interesting?" Thoroughly intrigued by the encounter, Sunny bought the book and began reading it as soon as she got back to her friend's home.

The introduction said the book was about shapeshifting. "What in the world is shapeshifting?" she wondered. "And why did that old woman think I'd want to know about it?"

Reading the first chapter, Sunny found out the term refers to the art of changing one's form at will. Shapeshifters assume that the energies of all living creatures are present within us. Believing animals possess wisdom that outstrips that of human beings, they see animals as a source of energy and inspiration. Shapeshifters engage in animal dances and rituals to heal others and to meet the spiritual needs of people in their communities.

She was fascinated. The book described how those who possess this ability can move between planes of reality. Known as shamans, they can extend their consciousness beyond that of ordinary human beings and control their movements in both inner as well as outer space. They serve as visionaries, magicians, mediators, power brokers, ceremonialists, artists, musicians, healers, teachers, and guides.

Within twenty-four hours she read the entire book. Then she checked out books from the library and scoured the bookstores for more information. All of her waking moments were filled with reading about shapeshifting and shamans.

The references explained that, even though shapeshifting is an ancient tradition, many indigenous people believe it lives on in our collective unconscious. The practice of shapeshifting exists today as a path to healing, spiritual growth, and foretelling the future.

She was surprised to learn that shapeshifting is common to the traditions of many nations. Among the people who embrace shapeshifting are Australian aborigines; the Celts; the Druids of England and Ireland; practitioners of Wicca in Europe and North America; the Sami in Norway and Iceland; numerous Native American tribes; the Huichols in Mexico; Indonesian, African, and South American medicine people; and the Tibetan Bon Pa.

Many Celtic legends involve shapeshifting and metamorphosis. Intriguing tales describe how shamans survived by assuming various shapes. Because they retained their human intelligence and memory throughout their many transmigrations, they kept getting wiser.

In a Celtic myth about longevity, for example, Tuan MacCarill survived his race by changing his shape. He lived through subsequent ages in the shapes of a stag, a wild boar, a hawk, and a salmon until he was caught by a fisherman and eaten. He was reborn in human form with full memory of all that had happened to him in past existences and an accumulated knowledge of several hundred years.

The Celtic story about Taliesin tells how he changed into many different creatures. His transformations were all explorations of deeper levels of consciousness he discovered through totem beasts. By shapeshifting, he became acquainted with all these forms. From each form he learned something of value. His final transformation was rebirth as a human being.

The Celtic retribution tale of Math describes how he punished Gwydion and Gilifaethwy for the rape of Goewin by changing them into deer, swine, and wolves. To compensate for their misdeed, they were forced to couple as male and female animals. By the time they were restored to human shape they had acquired deep wisdom.

Some stories illustrate how shamans use shapeshifting to survive in situations where possessing a human form is dangerous. One such story describes the pursuit of St. Patrick by King Loegaire's troops. St. Patrick invoked a charm which changed him and his monks into the shape of deer so they could escape.

Sunny learned that Celtic deities typically assume three forms. The Goddess of War and patroness of shapeshifting was Morrighan, later known as Morgan le Fay. Simultaneously she was Queen of Avalon, a healer, and a witch. Other goddesses are thought to be capable of shifting from the shape of a maiden to a matron and to a withered old woman.

After reading all of the books and articles about shamans and shape-shifting she could find, Sunny made a list of questions. Then she dialed the number the old woman had given her. Before the phone rang on the other end, the woman picked up the receiver. "I have been waiting for your call. We have a lot to talk about. Meet me tomorrow afternoon at three o'clock. I'll be in the same place where you last saw me."

Eager to find out more about shapeshifting, Sunny arrived early. When she saw the old woman slowly walking toward her, Sunny was beside herself with excitement. "I can't tell you how much I've been looking forward to talking with you!" she said. "I have learned so much from reading about shapeshifting. Please tell me more about this mysterious capability."

They sat down on a bench nearby. The old woman smiled gently and responded, "In the Native American tradition the crow is a shapeshifter and omen of change. We believe it has knowledge of the mysteries of creation and protects ancient records. So you see, to have 'crow's feet' is not such a bad thing."

From her readings Sunny knew shamans could become crows, as well as a number of other entities. She asked, "Have you personally witnessed a shaman taking different shapes?"

The woman said, "Frequently, shamans will transform themselves into crows but they aren't limited to this shape. By nature, they are polymorphs. This means they can cross insurmountable barriers and assume the shapes of all sorts of living things . . . animals, birds, vegetables, rocks, roots, streams, leaves, wind, stars, roads, and waves. Because they can tap into the life force that's in everything, they can function willfully in the realms of non-ordinary reality.

"When I was a little girl the shaman in our tribe used shapeshifting as a way to petition for a successful hunt. First, he would contact the animal to be hunted by dressing in its skins and acting out its movements and sounds in a very elaborate dance. Once he thoroughly identified with it, he would summon the animal and request its sacrifice to ensure the continued existence of our tribe."

Having read about female shamans in the Celtic tradition and witches in both Europe and the United States, Sunny knew that people believed certain women were able to assume whatever shapes they pleased. She was curious about the old woman's experience with female shamans. She broached this subject.

"Were shamanic powers confined to men in your tribe?" she asked. The old woman laughed as she said, "No, not at all. We had a medicine woman who met many of the spiritual needs of our community and was just as powerful as the male shaman. She could shift into animal and plant form to learn healing practices and to communicate with the divine for guidance. She carried out healing rituals for those who were sick and performed animal dances to protect mothers and their babies during childbirth."

Sunny wanted to know what the old woman had to say about the relevance of shapeshifting in today's world. She asked, "How is shapeshifting useful to those of us alive today who aren't shamans?"

The old woman closed her eyes and went into deep thought. Then she replied, "Don't be so eager to deny your power. You have more in common with shamans than you know, but I'll get back to that later. Let me answer your question this way. You live in a complex world made up of many cultures. A skilled shapeshifter functions well in all of these worlds, simultaneously."

"So modern shapeshifting is about flexibility?" asked Sunny. "It enables someone to adapt, kind of like a chameleon?"

The old woman drew closer to Sunny and whispered, "The more you know about personal transformation, the better you can adapt to any kind of change. And adapting to change is essential to survival.

"Think about the skills you have already developed. You go through a transformation every time you go to work, come home, visit relatives, and entertain friends. Knowing how to shift gracefully into each of these different realms is a preliminary stage of shapeshifting. As you acquire the conscious ability to become something different, more complex transitions will become easier."

Sunny was aware the woman was no longer speaking in generalities. The intensity of her gaze had increased. It was time to find out what was really on the woman's mind. Sunny said, "All of this is extremely interesting. But you seem to believe there's a reason why you and I have met that goes beyond simply talking about the subject of shapeshifting."

The old woman's eyes sparkled and she smiled knowingly. "Ah, at last we get to the real purpose of our meeting. You want to know how all this 'mumbo-jumbo' relates to you, personally. That's fair enough.

"Even though you aren't completely aware of what you are doing, you are choosing a new path. As a modern shapeshifter, you are making it a practice to fully enter each episode on your journey. Whenever you leave one place and adapt to a new set of circumstances, you are experiencing what it means to change your shape. Flowing like a river, you are learning how to move with natural ease through a wide variety of people, customs, environments, and energies.

"The path of a modern shapeshifter does not call for a change in your physical shape. What it does require is that you learn how to change your consciousness, at will. This means you must increase your ability to identify with other living creatures.

"This higher level of consciousness is essential to shapeshifting. It will enable you to appreciate that everything in creation is endowed with life, that divinity is implicit in all life, and that every form of life is worthy of respect and reverence."

Sunny was totally unprepared for what the old woman was revealing. "I find it difficult to understand what you're telling me. I certainly wasn't aware that I was choosing such a difficult path," she said.

The old woman continued, "Yes, it is a difficult path but it is also a wonderful path. Shapeshifting enables you to expand your perspective and to gain a deeper awareness of what's going on around you. It provides a gateway to other worlds. As a modern shapeshifter, you will experience many realities."

Sunny remembered the woman's comment about shamans. "What did you mean when you said I shared something in common with shamans?" Sunny asked. "From what I've read they are a lot like wizards. Don't they perform magic?"

"And now for the part about shamans," said the old woman. "I'm glad I can help you find the path you have been searching for. You are destined to fulfill a very special purpose—to become a contemporary shaman.

"To awaken the shaman within you must understand your purpose in life. Then you need to accept your place in the circle. From this position you will guide, inspire, enliven, and fill with spirit everything that surrounds you. You will liberate people from suffering, awaken their compassion, strengthen their minds, and lead them to supreme knowledge.

"Recently, some secrets were revealed while you were experiencing different realities. Stay open to new realities; more secrets will be revealed. Revelations may come through things you see in a dream, a reverie, or a trance. You may have visions while you are daydreaming or while you are in a state of ecstasy.

"As you awaken the shaman inside, you will witness changes within yourself and in your surroundings. You will learn how to alter the circumstances of your day-to-day existence. You will be empowered to cross barriers that are normally insurmountable.

"Your journey is demonstrating that borders aren't as substantial as you once thought they were. In the eyes of a shaman, the border between an individual and other life forms isn't solid. Nor is there a rigid boundary between matter and spirit. As a contemporary shaman, you will heal others by helping them establish a relationship between the world of matter and the world of spirit.

"In addition to healing individuals, you will heal the community. You will show people how to regain their power so they can bring about social and economic change."

While the old woman was talking, Sunny was aware of tears welling up in her own eyes. Here was the direction she sought. And even though she knew the magnitude of responsibility associated with being a shaman was awesome, she was deeply moved by what the woman said.

Sunny fumbled around in her purse for a handkerchief. Blotting her eyes, she took a deep breath to regain her composure, then looked up. To her utter disbelief, the old woman was nowhere to be seen. She had disappeared!

That evening Sunny called the old woman. All she got was a message that the number had been disconnected. There was no forwarding number.

Sunny Learns to Shapeshift

Sunny heard about a new metaphysical bookstore in a small town nearby. Gambling that she would find more references to shapeshifting, she drove over to check it out. The trip paid off! She located a thick volume containing lots of new information.

This book explained how shapeshifting can take place in several different ways. At a very basic level it involves the ability to mimic. Talented actors are able to convey an illusion that they're someone or something else, even without wearing costumes or using props.

At an intermediate level shapeshifting means taking on the characteristics of those whose patterns a shapeshifter wants to adopt; that is, learning to speak, act, walk, and think like they do. Adopting the patterns of others requires one to be open and receptive. The key to success at this level is the ability to establish rapport.

Advanced shapeshifting is based on resonance—a sympathetic vibration of energy. Seasoned shapeshifters are empowered by the belief that everyone and everything projects an energy pattern. They learn how to merge with the energy pattern of something, know it from the inside, and change it from the inside by directed intent.

Advanced shapeshifting involves six steps. First, shapeshifters identify the change they want to make in a person, animal, or thing. Second, they establish a ritual to maintain their own centers and purposes to prevent the other entity from co-opting and absorbing them. Third, they learn how to merge with the entity's energy pattern. Fourth, they bring about the desired change in themselves. Fifth, they direct their intent toward changing the entity. In the sixth step, the entity changes in order to mirror the change the shapeshifters have undergone.

Reading about the different levels of shapeshifting enabled Sunny to appreciate the old woman's observations. Throughout her journey Sunny had made it a practice to be open and receptive. She had established rapport by adapting to the lifestyles of her hosts and by looking at the world through their eyes. Both her thoughts and her actions had become more diverse. Without making a conscious effort to do so, she was learning the basics of shapeshifting at an intermediate level.

One evening, while Sunny was thinking about shapeshifting and her journey, it occurred to her that she was developing an ability to assume five different shapes. She labeled these shapes an Organizer, a Strategist, a Communicator, a Bridge, and a Friend of Gaia (Mother Earth). Then she composed a brief description of each one and identified a situation in which she had assumed that shape.

AN ORGANIZER

An Organizer combines the attributes of a perfect wife and an Indian chief, both of whom command respect through their wisdom and managerial skills. This shape enables you to direct many projects simultaneously, keep others motivated, maintain stability, provide grounding, offer guidance, clear away debris, and make sense of confusion.

As you utilize your skills to build strong infrastructures, introduce form and order, conduct research, and maintain records, other people are able to put a lot of their actions on automatic. They trust that someone else is paying attention to details.

While visiting the couple who owned the jewelry store, Sunny assumed the shape of an Organizer. She brought order to their business by creating an office and an infrastructure that included a method of accounting and a filing system.

A STRATEGIST

A Strategist finds it easy to design plans, set goals, prioritize objectives, and follow through on implementation. You know that competition can add fun, zest, and excitement to everyday activities. You are pragmatic, efficient, and results-oriented.

This shape equips you to make predictions, design and use instruments, assemble parts, and build superior machines. You understand that people do a better job at complex tasks than do machines. You employ technology where it works and you get inappropriate technology out of the way.

A Strategist sees reality as a series of linear progressions. In this shape you rely on "if . . . then" thinking to make decisions and solve problems. You use short-term actions to achieve long-term goals.

Sunny's contribution to the owners of the small manufacturing firm that sold earthquake equipment was as a Strategist. She helped them draft a plan, establish objectives, and adopt tools to measure their progress.

A COMMUNICATOR

A Communicator is motivated by learning, likes to engage in dialogue, has a voracious appetite for data, and devotes a lot of time to receiving and passing on information. Because information comes from so many sources and not all of it is useful, a Communicator uses computers to help manage the flood of input.

In this shape you regard disorder and redundancy as desirable. You understand that information is complex, ever-expanding, and impossible to completely control.

Sunny's networking endeavors on behalf of the brew pub owners permitted her to take the shape of a Communicator. She applied her highly developed listening skills to obtain feedback. Then she used the information she received to help the owners increase the effectiveness of their outreach efforts.

A BRIDGE

A Bridge joins people, ideas, and resources. In this shape you negotiate boundaries, find common ground, and invigorate relationships. A Bridge works as a cultural broker at the interface between political, racial, religious, and social groups. Your efforts are based on what's best for others, not on your own need for control.

As a Bridge, you are both separated and connected, definite and indefinite, assertive and nurturant, tender and strong. You accept both change and stability, focus on both processes and goals, pursue both inner harmony and worldly success, and appreciate both the real and the ideal. A Bridge asks questions and provides answers, looks for order while adapting to change, and savors the richness of both absolute and relative truth. You search for cause at the same time you are searching for meaning. You draw upon both conventional wisdom and intuition.

Sunny served as a Bridge between the community of women and those in need of their services. More people were given assistance and the community was enriched as a result of her efforts.

A FRIEND OF GAIA

Assuming this shape allows you to see the Earth as a grand provider. You enjoy being outdoors and gain energy from the life force in nature. As a combination of Johnny Appleseed and The Corn Mother, this shape predisposes you to plant seeds of ideas everywhere and to regard the growth and development of children as a source of amazement and delight.

Responding to others' pain, a Friend of Gaia promotes healing and seeks justice. In this shape you find the study of other cultures personally fulfilling. A strong dedication to ecology prompts you to support causes that affect the health of the planet. As an ecological evangelist, you view spirituality as the highest form of political consciousness. You regard evil as an absence of light and make a conscious effort to embody light.

Sunny assumed the shape of a Friend of Gaia while she was visiting the organic farmers. She connected her hosts with people around the world who want to work in the best interest of the planet.

Five Organizational Shapes

For three weeks Sunny mulled over ideas about her work experiences, the lifestyles of people she'd met on her trip, and the five shapes she was learning to assume. She began to see how the shapes of organizations differ, depending on their function. She identified five possibilities and wrote brief descriptions of them. What follows are snapshots of five organizational shapes and their functions.

Organizational Shapes and Functions	
Shape	**Function**
Pyramid	Contract-Based
Arrow	Market-Driven
Web	Information-Oriented
Mosaic	Community-Focused
Sphere	Life-Centered

ORGANIZATIONS AS PYRAMIDS

When organizations are contract-based they assume the shape of pyramids. Binding agreements, with terms and conditions, draw people together in a hierarchy. Obligations, specifications, restrictions, principles, and regulations become important. Protocol, seniority, loyalty, and stability are emphasized.

Form and fit are critical. Form has to do with the configuration of buildings and offices, meeting the expectations of people above you, abiding by the accepted modes of communication, following orders, and completing documents. Fit refers to demonstrating a good job-person match, reflecting a corporate image, behaving according to the norms of a work group, and complying with established practices. When people or things don't fit the traditional mold, they are frequently rejected.

Jobs are compartmentalized. Employees compile charts, rely on checklists, and keep records. Progress is monitored through inspections, status updates, schedule reviews, and performance appraisals.

The leaders exercise control through policies, standard procedures, rules, and edicts. At the top of the pyramid, they make the major decisions then pass the word down through structured meetings and official communication channels.

Members of pyramid organizations often regard each other as family members. Leaders may act as benevolent parents by looking out for the best interests of the employees who depend on them, or they may serve as father figures by helping younger employees move up the corporate ladder.

ORGANIZATIONS AS ARROWS

Market-driven organizations are like arrows in that they are pointed in a specific direction. The objective is to gain market share. The focus is on competitive analysis and strategy.

Action, expediency, competition, achievement, and speed become critical because these organizations typify life in the fast lane. Setting goals and objectives, solving problems, achieving milestones, and maintaining a fast cycle time are key considerations. Everyone is under tremendous pressure to bring forth the latest products at the least cost in the shortest amount of time.

These organizations are designed to function like smooth-running economic machines. Engineers are revered. Managers are master mechanics who are responsible for harnessing technology in order to gain control of markets. To gain entry into these exclusive enclaves requires people to demonstrate that they possess a high level of technological expertise. Typically, this means having established a track record at a competing firm. Methodical, sequential approaches and flow charts give testimony to a linear perspective. There are lines of authority, methods for tracking product alignment, and frequent references to the bottom line. Assembly line workers engage in routine, repetitive tasks. Products compete on the basis of linear, cumulative data such as price, size, volume, durability, and push.

For high achievers and Type A people, work provides an avenue to prove self-worth. Meeting challenges and measuring up are ways to demonstrate professional prowess. To succeed, members must have staying power and not be afraid of confrontation. Successful performance also depends on making accurate predictions, meeting objectives, knowing the answers to key questions, outwitting opponents, and seizing the spotlight.

Competing successfully means being number one, both in terms of corporate standing and an individual's ranking. Since there are many people who want to be winners, members have to strategize about ways to get ahead of the pack. Working in this setting requires members to push themselves to the edge, blast a way to new opportunities, and punch through to meet their career goals.

ORGANIZATIONS AS WEBS

Information-oriented organizations assume the shape of webs. Web organizations are self-generating, self-managing, and self-destructing. In contrast with frozen structures they hang together, loosely, on the basis of networks and processes. Their boundaries are extremely permeable because they depend on a continual exchange of data.

The most important element is communication. Each network member is simultaneously connected at many points to a vast array of other people. Network members continually transmit data, exchange ideas, and solicit feedback.

Productivity depends on the members' abilities to anticipate what is coming, move information through the system to those who need it, eliminate cracks where data could fall through, respond to corrective feedback, and learn from experience. High performers are those who gain access to accurate information, correctly interpret it, and use it wisely. Cross-training ensures overlapping skills and increases individual flexibility.

Members of web organizations understand that services exist only in time, so they make an effort to serve customers in real-time. They standardize their products and customize their services to ensure customer satisfaction.

Within web organizations informal communication tends to be extremely imaginative. Members value their work because it provides links and enables them to be knowledgeable about a wide range of topics. They are encouraged to explore new approaches, even in regard to routine tasks. Individuals have a great deal of control over their work and many of them work from home.

ORGANIZATIONS AS MOSAICS

When organizations are community-focused they assume the shape of mosaics. In mosaic organizations a wide variety of people come together to form a whole. These organizations acquire a pattern of their own, based on a shared vision and commonly held beliefs and values.

One of the goals of mosaic organizations is to enlarge the playing field for everyone. Everyone benefits as the success of the community accelerates.

Believing that boundaries are created for convenience, the community members appreciate the importance of both solitude and togetherness. They value both autonomy and collaboration.

The members believe that individual rights and needs must be connected to a sense of social responsibility. They develop avenues for self-expression at the same time they are participating in group projects. A major theme is, "I'll get my part done while I ensure that we get the group project done, too."

Strong bonds grow from mutual respect. Group members make an effort to understand how other people are thinking and feeling. Diversity is seen as a resource. The members seek harmony by working to achieve consensus and by regarding their differences as sources of innovation.

In mosaic organizations work offers a way to unite in community around a common purpose. Members regard work as a service. It is something they do to make a contribution and it is integrated with the rest of their lives.

Members assume if they serve a larger good, economic benefits will follow. They also believe that cooperation can lead to economic and social results that are superior to other alternatives. Ownership rights are gained by active participation rather than through financial investment.

There are few set roles; everyone learns how to do many things. High performance is achieved through integration, cohesion, synergy, and group bonding. Members reward each other for integrity, authenticity, spontaneity, improvisation, and imagination.

ORGANIZATIONS AS SPHERES

Organizations that are life-centered assume the shape of spheres. As spheres, organizations resemble very basic biological organisms. They have no skeletons; consequently, they have extremely flexible structures. They are held together by world-wide partnerships based on ties that transcend national borders.

Spheres do away with boundaries, help people gain broader perspectives, and foster a sense of connection among living creatures. How to strengthen one's relationship with the environment is a key consideration.

Members look upon everyone and everything on the Earth as equally distant from the center at all points. At the center is the source of life.

Cross-pollination is key as people seek new ways to do everything, drawing upon practices and customs from around the world. Members form consortiums and liaisons that resemble packets of energy with the potential to explode into new, creative ventures.

In spheres, people are motivated by a desire to make a difference. Instead of asking, "What is the problem?" members ask, "What are we going to do to make this world a better place?" They provide expertise and materials that enable households and businesses to become energy independent. They work to ensure restoration and preservation of the natural environment. They support causes linked to human rights and economic justice. And they sponsor convocations to explore alternative scenarios for the future.

Circles of Influence

After Sunny finished writing the descriptions of five organizational shapes, an image began to form in her mind. She saw there was a connection between individual shapes and the shapes that organizations assume.

Five Individual and Organizational Shapes	
Individual Shape	**Organizational Shape**
Organizer	Pyramid
Strategist	Arrow
Communicator	Web
Bridge	Mosaic
Friend of Gaia	Sphere

She also saw that the connection between these two types of shapes is dynamic. Through a process of co-evolution, each calls forth the other.

**The Co-Evolution of Individual
and Organizational Shapes**

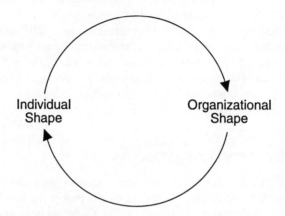

ORGANIZERS AND PYRAMIDS

Organizers build structures based on position, policies, procedures, protocol, and best practices. They produce and support hierarchies by categorizing and ranking people and things. Pyramids attract and produce Organizers in the roles of commanders, overseers, administrators, researchers, and specialists.

STRATEGISTS AND ARROWS

Strategists produce and support arrow-shaped organizations that are aimed at specific target niches. To beat the competition, arrow-shaped organizations attract and produce Strategists in the roles of champions, heroes and conquerors, diplomats, power brokers, tacticians, catalysts, and coaches of all-star teams.

COMMUNICATORS AND WEBS

Communicators produce and support organizational webs by continually exchanging information with other members of their networks. Webs attract and produce Communicators in the roles of educators, guides, facilitators, navigators, translators, webmasters, and computer junkies.

BRIDGES AND MOSAICS

Due to their affinity for eliminating boundaries and bringing elements together, Bridges produce and support organizations in the shape of mosaics. Mosaics attract and produce Bridges in the roles of reframers, boundary negotiators, consensus builders, mediators, matchmakers, impresarios, and synthesizers.

FRIENDS OF GAIA AND SPHERES

Friends of Gaia perceive the center of the Earth as the source of life and all forms of creation as sacred. As they join with others around the world in an effort to sustain the planet, they produce and support organizations that assume the shape of spheres. Spheres attract and produce Friends of Gaia in the role of "bioneers," pioneers who specialize in finding practical solutions for restoring the environment. Spheres also serve as meeting grounds for evangelists, stewards, visionaries, map makers, world travelers, and global citizens who make it a practice to live lightly on the Earth.

THE DEVELOPMENT OF SANDBOXES

Thinking about the five organizational shapes and the conversations between the two sandboxes, Sunny realized that most sandboxes probably start out as pyramids and arrows. As these organizations grow and develop, their negative aspects are given a wide berth. While their dark sides expand, their light sides shrink.

Over a long period of time both kinds of organizations become closed and rigid. Ultimately, they reach a point where any type of dissent is perceived as a lack of loyalty; any form of innovation is regarded as a threat. In their struggle to move up and get ahead of the pack, people become suspicious of love and compassion. What were once functional systems become dysfunctional.

"Why does this happen?" Sunny wondered. "How are these organizational systems able to expand without any checks and balances?"

Then it came to her. Human beings opt out of the process as co-creators. For the most part, they live out the sandboxes' stories and totally neglect their own.

She saw how the circular relationship between individuals and organizational systems can be both healthy and unhealthy. In the healthy circle we write our own life stories then we create organizational systems to support our stories. These systems come into being and assume their own identities in the form of stories. As we write new stories for ourselves we are influenced by the systems' stories. This process continues in a cyclical manner.

In an unhealthy circle we write our stories and create systems to support them. The systems come into being, develop their own stories, and influence our stories. But instead of writing new stories of our own, we relinquish our place in the circle and conform to the systems' stories.

With the passage of time we completely forget how to write our own stories and how to create systems to support our stories.

A Healthy Circle of Influence

We write our stories.

We create systems to support our stories.

Systems come into their stories.

Systems shape our stories.

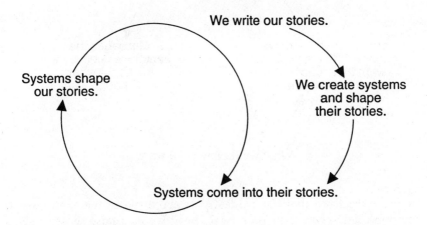

An Unhealthy Circle of Influence

We write our stories.

We create systems and shape their stories.

Systems come into their stories.

Systems shape our stories.

Thinking about the circles of influence Sunny surmised, "In spite of all of the posturing, boasting, and chest-beating pronouncements I witnessed on the part of the two sandboxes, the truth is that we humans keep them going. They are animate because we enliven them. Without our energy they would cease to exist."

During her reverie in the dentist's office the sandboxes had admitted as much. She remembered how they acknowledged that, in spite of their being able to take on identities of their own, they depend on the time, talents, and allegiance of people to bring them to life and sustain them.

"Why do we give away our energy without asking for more, in return?" Sunny asked herself. "And why do we surrender our place in the circle?"

According to what the sandboxes said, human beings give up power in exchange for protection and security. Humans prefer the safety of boxes to the risk of the unknown.

"What the sandboxes concluded has merit," she thought. "But I think the time has come for us to make a cold, hard appraisal of what we have lost in this bargain. By relinquishing our power, we're required to adopt the sandboxes' stories as our own. Day after day we accept roles that fit their plots, read from their scripts, and go after what they tell us we want and need."

Sunny labeled the process of adopting the sandboxes' stories as our own, "A Cycle of Conformity." She drew a loop depicting how the sandboxes influence our thoughts and actions in order to ensure their own longevity.

A Cycle of Conformity

The sandboxes' stories

Actions, behaviors we engage in to get what we want that support the sandboxes' existence

Messages the sandboxes convey to us about what we (should) want

What we (believe we) want

Sunny realized that the saddest part about life in the sandboxes is they don't deliver on their promises. They give us a false sense of security. When they fail to provide safe havens, we suffer from being left out in the cold. And because the glow of being in the winner's circle fades quickly, we must constantly strive to achieve new goals and objectives.

Taking stock of her progress, Sunny was pleased with everything she had learned thus far. "At the very least I will no longer contribute energy to perpetuating the existence of the sandboxes," she reassured herself. "And with any luck I'll find a way to change them."

A Teller of Tales

One avenue to changing the sandboxes would be to go back and examine their ancestral roots. What grand legacy might they have inherited? If she knew the full stories of their heritage, perhaps she could devise a way to restore their light sides.

She recalled the old woman's words, "The energies of all living creatures are present within you. You simply have to tap them."

Trusting that what the woman had said was true, Sunny concluded, "The sandboxes are examples of two organizational shapes—a pyramid and an arrow. If I regard these shapes as living entities, I ought to be able to tap their energies inside me. And while I'm at it, I'll ask the other three shapes to tell me their stories. That way, I'll have ideas about alternatives."

Assuming she could establish enough rapport to connect with the five organizational shapes, she went into a deep meditative state. Then she asked each of them, in turn, "If you could speak, what would you say? Please tell me your story."

Over a period of several weeks all five shapes responded by telling their stories. She recorded these tales as they came to her. Then she began passing on the stories to promote awareness of how organizations represent a variety of realities. She looked upon this effort as a precursor to a more encompassing project that would involve changing the sandboxes and creating new organizational systems.

"Part Two: Tales of Five Realities" is an account of the stories as Sunny recorded them. Each story depicts the grand reality on which its corresponding organizational shape is based.

The Relationship Between Realities, Organizational Shapes and Sandboxes

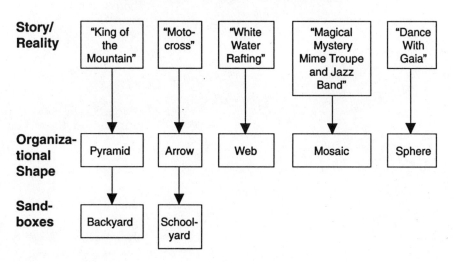

Story/Reality	"King of the Mountain"	"Moto-cross"	"White Water Rafting"	"Magical Mystery Mime Troupe and Jazz Band"	"Dance With Gaia"
Organizational Shape	Pyramid	Arrow	Web	Mosaic	Sphere
Sandboxes	Backyard	Schoolyard			

PART TWO

Tales of Five Realities

Learning to live with many points of view, many different ways of experiencing reality, is perhaps the greatest challenge of the new, complex society in which we find ourselves.

DANAH ZOHAR AND IAN MARSHALL
The Quantum Society

Reality is only a consensual hunch.

LILY TOMLIN

4. The Pyramid

King of the Mountain

Once upon a time there was a king named Rem who lived in a large castle on top of a high mountain. He was married to a charming wife and they had a beautiful daughter. Fifty ministers, twelve scribes, twenty gatekeepers, and ten servants served him faithfully.

The castle was surrounded by a moat so big the royal boats could sail on it. Anyone needing to conduct official business had to get permission from one of the gatekeepers in order to cross the drawbridge.

The kingdom was surrounded by a granite wall, twenty feet thick and thirty feet tall, that was covered with slippery moss. Only those who lived on the mountain were able to see over it. This wall protected those inside from intruders but it also kept them isolated.

Without exception, the ruling monarchs had always been sure they were doing everything right so they saw no need to rely on people outside the wall for anything. Those inside the wall were assumed to be allies. Those outside were regarded as foreigners and potential enemies.

King Rem delighted in taking his meals outdoors on one of the many balconies so he could survey his property and look down on the countryside where the villagers lived and worked. He was proud to say he had a good life.

Such had not always been the case; he was born and raised in the lowlands. Unlike monarchs who come into power through inheritance, King Rem gained access to the throne by being a fierce warrior. Time after time he was victorious in battle. He defended the kingdom and significantly increased the territory over which his predecessor reigned.

After each victory Rem was rewarded with property on the mountain. Finally, as the king's most trusted ally, he was invited to occupy rooms in the castle. When the king was about to die without a male heir, he crowned Rem as his successor.

Upon his ascent to the throne, King Rem appointed one brother Minister of Finance, made a second brother Minister of Resource Allocation, and promoted a third brother to the position of Minister of Justice. Reporting to these three senior ministers were vice ministers, associate ministers, and assistant ministers.

Excellence was measured on the basis of previous accomplishments. Any changes to the standard procedures required the king's signature, but only the Minister of Signatures could gain an audience with the king for this purpose. Since this minister met with King Rem for only fifteen minutes every month, very few procedures changed.

The laws of the land had been laid down many years before. Everyone assumed no matter who ruled, the precedents that had been established would continue to exist. The fundamental laws were these:

Pay homage to the king.
Honor the past.
Respect your superiors.
Don't question authority.
When in doubt, ask for permission.

The king expected his subjects to know the laws and to obey them without question. In the event of a violation, justice was swift. Violators were quickly apprehended and locked in the castle tower until they came before a court-appointed magistrate. If found guilty, they could be banished from the kingdom. Fortunately, there had been few times in the history of this village when such a severe measure had to be used. In most cases violators were permitted to remain in the village; nevertheless, they were marked with earcuffs.

The king was proud of the fact that there was so little friction throughout the kingdom. His subjects adhered closely to the traditional ways, followed the established rituals, and performed as loyal citizens. He was certain that most people felt safe and secure as a result of the stability and order they had come to expect. He liked to think of the people in the valley as extensions of his own family. In many ways they were like his children—dependent and in need of protection. He saw himself as a stern father, responsible for their well-being.

Due to the pyramidal structure of power and influence, members of the court received many more benefits than did commoners. Rights differed depending on economic status and social position. The higher one's status, the closer one lived to the castle. It was only natural, therefore, that many people wanted to move from their small plots in the valley to estates located higher up the mountain.

One legitimate way to move up was to become a war hero. By fending off intruders, destroying invaders, and acquiring possessions and territory in the name of the king, a warrior could advance in rank and significantly increase his privileges. Men who demonstrated military valor and skill received lifetime compensation for service to the throne. Those who engaged in acts of distinguished bravery were given land on the mountain on which to build their homes.

Women were never recognized as valiant because they couldn't serve as soldiers. Unless they happened to be members of the royal family or were lucky enough to marry heroes, they could never hope to increase their status and position. Nor could servants or serfs who were destined to put in long hours cooking, cleaning, and toiling in the fields.

For the most part the villagers accepted their lot. They were accustomed to their daily routines and regularly went about their business. Things were so predictable, some villagers complained of being bored. But no matter how mundane their activities, they all looked forward to certain official occasions.

King Rem took pride in the number of gala events he introduced during his reign. Artists, musicians, actors, and comedians were kept busy planning ceremonies to which all of the villagers were invited. The king said it was important to channel talent so it was of benefit to all. But he secretly believed that too much creativity could be a dangerous thing. By sponsoring the special events, he could control the way creativity was expressed.

The most popular part of these events was the lottery sponsored by the Ministers of Education and Religion. Winning the lottery meant being eligible for an annual drawing in which the top winner was awarded two slaves who had been captured as prisoners in previous battles. Nearly everyone entered because it offered a ray of hope that perhaps, someday, their luck would change.

Because King Rem had a daughter rather than a son, he had to take steps to locate an heir. He decided to create a challenge whereby some young man could prove himself worthy to rule the kingdom. King Rem proclaimed throughout the land that he was deeply troubled by a mysterious threat of impending evil. He decreed that the man who eliminated this danger would marry the princess and be crowned the heir apparent.

The townspeople found the king's proclamation puzzling; he appeared to have everything under control. The king's soldiers had proven to be superior on the few occasions when the kingdom was attacked by wandering hordes.

Little did they know the king had a secret. Before his mother died, she warned him of a giant who lived in a cave not far away. Due to a troll's curse, the giant had been asleep for two hundred years. He was destined to awaken within the current year. For all the king knew, the giant could be stalking the countryside. The king was certain that his forces would be powerless against the mighty giant but he didn't want to worry the people who were under his protection.

At the foot of the mountain lived a widow with her youngest son, Erik. Two older sons had proven their physical prowess in military campaigns. The eldest was knighted for his ability on the battlefield. Because he was also a superb craftsman, he redesigned the moat so it afforded the castle more protection. He created new weaponry, invented better tools, and added amenities to make life in the castle more pleasant. For his service he was given land on which to build a home on the north side of the mountain.

The middle son had also been knighted. He led many battles and emerged victorious. In recognition of his leadership he was awarded the coveted Sword of Bravery and given land for a home on the south side of the mountain.

Erik admired his two older brothers and wanted to be just as successful as they. He dreamed of becoming a knight. But his father died unexpectedly, leaving Erik to manage the farm. In spite of his dreams, Erik felt pressured to assume responsibility for the farm and take care of his mother.

One day while Erik was hunting for game in the woods he heard a raspy voice repeating something over and over. He dismounted and moved quietly through the bushes to find out who was making such strange sounds. To his utter amazement, he discovered it was a troll. The creature was singing:

The thing the king wants the most
Is to be in a position to boast
That the giant is dead.
Someone cut off his head;
And to this great hero he'll toast!

Erik knew that trolls possess supernatural power so he did not want to come face to face with the creature. He made his way back to his horse, quickly mounted, and rode home.

The next evening while his mother was fixing dinner, he described the troll's song and asked what it could mean. She confided that years ago she had overheard her mother talking with a friend about a sleeping giant. This giant was destined to awaken after two hundred years. The friend had told the story with fear and trepidation because she assumed the giant would seek revenge when he awoke. There was no telling what he might do to release his anger and ease his hunger.

Erik's mother thought the troll's song indicated the giant was no longer asleep. He was probably on the move, looking for food. The troll also seemed to know that, at some point, the giant would be killed by a person brave enough to cut off the giant's head.

Anything that might pose a threat to his mother triggered Erik's sense of responsibility. And so, he decided he must put an end to the evil giant. But before he could cut off the giant's head he would have to learn how to use a sword.

Erik's older brothers were happy to serve as instructors and they agreed to keep the mission a secret. Erik practiced diligently until his brothers assured him he was the best swordsman in the land. At last he was ready.

One morning he awoke before dawn and rode off to meet his fate. He kept going until he was so tired he could go no further. Fortunately, at that point he came upon what appeared to be a deserted cottage. He stopped to rest and fell into a deep sleep on a bed of straw.

He awoke with a start and was horrified to see the troll sitting in front of him. Wanting to get away before the troll could work an evil spell, he tried to escape. But the troll spoke reassuringly, saying,

The giant sleeps all through the day.
Here's a map to show you the way.
For the room where he'll be,
You'll need this gold key.
No matter the cost; it's him you must slay.

Erik set out to accomplish his mission. He rode over hill and dale without meeting anyone. At dusk he came upon a splendid castle. He knocked at the door. It was opened by an old man with hair as white as snow. Erik asked for a night's lodging. The old man said he was welcome to stay on the condition that he understood the castle belonged to a wicked giant. This evil being had plundered the old man's village and taken him prisoner to be a servant.

Erik explained the purpose of his journey. Aware that a potential liberator had arrived, the old man prepared a tasty meal. Erik ate, then made his way to a small room under the stairs where he fell fast asleep.

The next morning the old man gently woke Erik, served him breakfast, and took him upstairs to the room where the giant was sleeping. Using the troll's gold key to unlock the door, Erik quietly tiptoed into the huge cavern of a room.

Gaining entry to the giant's chambers was the easy part, however. The giant had a built-in defensive maneuver. Each time Erik tried to approach the gigantic bed the giant snored and exhaled in a tremendous rush of air that forced the young man back against the wall.

Erik was distraught. Had he come this far for nothing? He had to find a way to get the giant to turn over without waking up.

At the very moment he was struggling to devise a plan, a hawk flew in through the window and landed on the giant's cheek. The bird slowly began to make its way toward the voluminous nostrils. All of a sudden the giant's great hulk of a hand came down on his own cheek as he sought to eliminate the bothersome pest. The hawk escaped in the nick of time. The giant let out a huge roar of a yawn and rolled over on his other side.

Erik waited until he was sure the giant was sound asleep. Then he silently made his way up to the side of the monstrous bed. There he stood until he could gather sufficient courage to strike the fatal blow. With an explosive burst of energy he brought his sword crashing down. His aim was true. The giant's head was cleanly separated from his body. And as Erik raced toward the door, he heard the head cursing him with its last breath.

King Rem was ecstatic when he learned of Erik's conquest. He threw a huge party to celebrate the victory and to announce the engagement of his daughter to the young hero.

All of this took Erik by surprise. Not only did he not know about the king's decree; he thought it would be foolish to marry a woman he didn't even know.

After a long negotiation process, the king agreed to give Erik and his mother a farm on the north side of the mountain. This farm was near Erik's oldest brother's home and next to a ranch owned by the favorite uncle of the princess. Erik agreed to marry the princess on the condition they became friends first.

The princess was accustomed to visiting her uncle regularly because he was a widower and she liked to cook his favorite meals. She extended her visits in order to spend time with Erik. The two young people began the process of getting to know each other. Erik taught her about farming. She introduced him to the traditions of courtly life. The uncle of the princess fell in love with Erik's mother and the two of them lived happily on their adjoining properties.

5. The Arrow

Motocross

It had happened. There was no doubt about it. Chris knew he was hooked. He had become a motorcycle junkie. The rush of adrenalin, the buzz, and the power surge that come from going into a curve, kissing the ground, then rocketing out of a turn—all of these called to him. He felt totally possessed.

Oddly enough, at the same time that he felt a creeping sense of addiction he experienced tremendous freedom. He could rev. He could make quick turns. He could let out all the stops. He could fly.

It was the sensation of flying that really hooked him. He never felt so in tune with nature as during those precious few moments when he seemed to transcend his human form and become a large bird, soaring in the blue, sun-warmed sky. For a short time he could operate in a totally different reality. He'd find himself chuckling as he thought to himself, "They don't call these machines 'Eagles' and 'Hawks' for nothing!"

Gradually he had worked his way up to a hyper-thumper with low end burst yet sedate enough to maintain traction. His bike combined ruggedness with comfort and power. It also rebounded quickly and was ready for the next hit a micro-second later.

Two years ago his friend, Randy, had convinced him that racing would open up a whole new appreciation for riding. Since then he'd learned how to have fun taking risks. Randy continually urged him to welcome hazards and take chances. "Let your machine run," Randy would say. "If you always have the brakes on you'll never learn how to deal with the next curve."

In a relatively short time he had gotten himself into excellent physical condition, significantly improved his skills, and increased his speed. Now the excitement and sheer terror of cross-country racing held him in its grasp. He found the sensation of being invincible tremendously exhilarating and he loved the afterglow.

Occasionally, he won a race but his focus wasn't on winning. Having learned that winning or losing is as much a gamble as it is skill-related, he took his losses in stride. Being able to go fast was a nice sideline to a fulfilling life but riding a motorcycle didn't define his value as a person. "No matter what the outcome," he told himself, "there will always be another day and another race."

At first he'd been a little put off at how everything about motocross was combative. Even the fans competed with each other for the best positions by the fence and for bragging rights after correctly predicting who would win. The competition was so intense that close friends were known to become enemies once they were on the track.

Randy was the most competitive biker Chris knew. In fact, Randy's whole identity was tied to winning motorcycle races. He set very specific objectives and carefully tracked his progress. Detailed charts on the walls of his apartment served as proof of his ability to meet his milestones. Each race was a clash for supremacy. Friendship, consideration, and good manners had no place in a barn-burner duel to the death.

Randy frequently admonished Chris for being too soft. In an effort to get Chris to toughen up Randy would say, "You have to want to win more than anything else. Get your purpose and goals straight. Very few of the other riders will. This gives you the advantage."

Everyone agreed Randy was an awesome performer. Years of dedication, combined with natural ability and incredible resolve, helped make him a champion. During his lifetime he had spent long hours learning how to ride well. Now he thought there was no greater reward for his efforts than victory.

He won most of the races he entered and his success made him arrogant. He took great delight in trying to intimidate other competitors even though he wasn't physically imposing. In his mind wanting to control bigger and better machines was no different from wanting to have power over other people. He would confide to Chris, "People are like sheep, man. You have to herd them. They only change as a knee-jerk reaction to something you do to them. You do them a favor by forcing them up against a wall. It helps them get clear about their priorities."

If Randy lost a race he'd be grouchy, angry, and depressed. He'd come up with some kind of excuse and blame the weather, the condition of the track, what somebody else had done in the race, or an equipment failure. A loss would force Randy's mood down so low that Chris would think he was suicidal.

Soon after meeting him Chris had come to accept the fact that motocross brought out the bully in Randy. He told Chris it was his "teeter-totter" philosophy. The way he put it was, "Whenever somebody else goes down I automatically go up a few notches."

Randy was always on the lookout for ways to beat the clock, the odds, and the competition. Occasionally his emphasis on beating everyone led to violence. He had a short fuse and was known to have decked people who openly disagreed with him. He justified his behavior by comparing motocross to combat: "When you enter a race, it's war—every man for himself to the finish line."

One of the most ironic things about Randy was that he really felt alive only when there was a chance he could be killed. He believed it was important to live on the edge and was proud of his ability to risk. If he thought Chris was being overly cautious he'd chide him, saying, "There's only so much time, man! The clock is winding down. You've go to make the most of each minute."

Chris had come to expect a complete personality change in his friend whenever they entered a race. Randy would shoot out from the start line like he was strapped to the nose of a Patriot missile. From that moment, until he crossed the finish line, he could pass for a Terminator clone. He became a formidable force, bent on wiping out anything and everything in his path.

To a certain extent Chris could understand Randy's intense desire to duke it out. His superior machinery manifested the ultimate in mach power. What puzzled Chris was how Randy would squeeze him off track, get sand in his eyes, and run over rocks so they'd be tossed back as flying projectiles, then be all smiles after the race.

Once Chris pointed out to Randy how totally different he was on and off the course. Randy's retort was, "Hey, man, get with the program! Out there you're in a war zone. It's dog-eat-dog! When we're racing you're an opponent I have to beat." Another time Chris complained because Randy nearly caused him to collide with a guard rail. Randy simply said, "What a blast! We were raging, man! I never had so much fun. Don't take it so personally."

After that incident Chris asked himself, "Why do I keep coming back for more?" The only way he could justify his own behavior was on the basis of Randy's personal magnetism. When he was with Randy he felt strong and self-confident. He also knew he tolerated Randy's arrogance because of his friend's knowledge of motorcycles and exceptional racing skills. He just couldn't help admiring Randy's ability.

* * *

Today was a really big event. Bikers had come from all over the United States to compete for the national championship title. There were four entrants who had won more races than Randy, so he was really jazzed. Winning this race would put him above some of the best.

But Chris had a bad feeling about this race. The night before, Randy confided that he didn't just intend to win the race. He planned to totally dominate all of the other bikers by leaving them in his wake. He told Chris how he would get launched by using a new hot start strategy and how he would triumph in the dogfight over the set of uphill jumps. If his high flying, cunning, and awesome skill meant others had to crash and burn, so be it.

Another friend of Randy's had entered this race—a man from out of town named Bruce. He seemed to be a nice, average guy, but he had a record that rivaled Randy's. Beneath a friendly facade lay the skill of an experienced opponent.

Randy's girlfriend, Patty, was also at the race. She was afraid of anything that smelled of hot oil and went fast, so she rarely came to watch Randy perform. But it was very important to have Patty there because Randy got his kicks from being seen as a daredevil champion by women. He'd made a deal with her. If she came to watch him ride he'd take her out for dinner and dancing. The race was timed, with two riders leaving every fifteen seconds. The four superior bikers were in the number one and two positions. Randy and Bruce were in third position. Chris was next to a guy from Oregon in tenth position. The race was about to begin. Randy looked back, flashed a big smile, and gave Chris a thumbs-up.

As soon as the official gave the signal to start the race, Randy began to play it mean and cold so the competition would understand he was no sissy. He revved hard and burst forward like he was taking off from an aircraft carrier. He got the holeshot and peppered Bruce with grains of sand. Then he tried to position his bike for encounters that would offer opportunities to hurt other bikers, break their bikes, and eliminate the competition.

It was a while before Chris got close enough to see what Randy was doing. Then he began to push himself, thinking, "This guy has really gone off the deep end!" He rode as hard as he could for the next ten minutes until he was nearly exhausted. But his endurance paid off.

He came upon Randy just as Bruce was passing him on the right, with a roar. Randy took off after Bruce in a rage. The two of them rampaged through the brush and over the rocks.

The next thing Chris knew, Bruce's wheel tucked under in a big sand berm. He went down. Then Randy hit Bruce's bike and crashed, flying over the two bikes and landing on top of Bruce. Neither of the men moved.

As soon as Chris reached the collision site he knew something was wrong. Randy was complaining that his legs hurt but Bruce was lying very still. Chris quickly dismounted. When he got close enough to touch Bruce he could tell the man wasn't breathing. Another rider came on the scene, jumped off of his bike, and began to administer CPR. Suddenly, Randy bolted up, jumped back on his motorcycle, and took off. The rider who was taking care of Bruce reported the injured man was breathing again. He urged Chris to get back in the race, saying he would stay with Bruce until the paramedics arrived.

Chris sensed a howling scream beginning to rise from deep inside. He wanted to protest the terrible injustice that he'd witnessed. Countless emotions rushed through his mind. He felt like he was going to explode. "Please let Bruce recover!" he kept thinking to himself.

He jumped up and eased himself into the saddle of his machine. His cautious nature gave way to raw anger. His purpose was focused like a laser beam. As the blood pulsed through his head he was overcome with a desire for revenge. All he could think was, "I must beat Randy."

Pure rage washed away his inhibitions. He felt a calm come over him as he let out all the stops. Riding faster than ever before, he realized why Randy was so addicted to the chase. The roar of his bike was intense. The brush was a blur as he sped faster and faster. Everything began to take on a surreal quality as he lost touch with what was reasonable and safe. He became one with his machine. Together they were unstoppable.

Eventually, he saw Randy up ahead. The horrible accident flashed before his eyes, spurring him on even faster. Soon the pebbles thrown up by the rear wheel of Randy's bike began to pelt his helmet and gloved hands. Randy tried to cut him off but was unsuccessful. Both riders snaked their way through the arid course at breakneck speed. Neither glanced at the other. They were consumed by the race. The dueling riders traded positions numerous times. Jockeying for position seemed to go on for an eternity. It was clear neither man intended to yield. Both men were exhausted and surviving on sheer determination and willpower.

At last, Chris saw the marker indicating the final stretch. Randy was in the lead, pulling away with each twist of the throttle. Chris knew if

Randy made the next jump it would be very difficult to beat him. His heart began to ache and his stomach tightened. Chris knew he had to win, both for Bruce and for himself.

Chris gave it all he had. He was beside Randy when the two of them took the final jump. Like majestic steel birds, they soared in perfect unison. In a split second both bikes came crashing back to earth. They had to make an instant turn to stay on the track. Chris landed smoothly and cleanly executed the turn. Randy's bike, however, landed a bit skewed. As he tried to make the turn, he crashed into a tree. His body came to an abrupt halt near a clump of brush.

Chris crossed the finish line victoriously. Enthusiastic fans carried him into the winner's circle where he was awarded the championship trophy. The roar of the crowd drowned out the sound of the other bikers finishing the race.

In place of jubilation he felt despair. The shouting and frenzied excitement of the crowd became a low, rumbling noise that he wanted desperately to escape. Bruce's accident, Randy's outrageous behavior, and his own temporary lack of regard for his own life had left him in shock. In a daze, he accepted the congratulations of well-wishers. Deep inside he knew he never wanted to race again.

Later, Chris heard that Bruce had suffered a broken arm and two bruised ribs but was expected to recover completely. Randy had broken both legs. Chris was elated when he heard that Bruce would be all right. He knew he should feel sorry that Randy was injured but he felt a total lack of sympathy. All he wanted to do was get right in Randy's face and say in a very loud voice, "Gee, man, don't take it so personally!"

✳ ✳ ✳

Twenty years later Chris faced a dilemma. His sixteen-year-old daughter wanted to learn how to ride a motorcycle in order to participate in motocross events. Given the fact that she was extremely headstrong, Chris knew he couldn't forbid her to ride. That would only force her to rebel.

After a series of heart-to-heart talks in which he told her the story of his victory over Randy, he agreed to teach her everything he knew about motorcycles and motocross races. She agreed she would strive to become the kind of rider who knows how to compete without doing others in.

6. The Web

White Water Rafting

Here she was, stranded beside the Salmon River in a sparsely populated area of Idaho in the company of a man with whom she thought she could communicate but who turned out to be insensitive and unpredictable. "How did I get myself in such a jam?" she wondered.

It all started when she joined a network of soccer fans who exchange news and information on an electronic bulletin board. Both he and she had played soccer in school and were passionate fans, as adults. After meeting at a Major League Soccer championship match, they began sending E-mail messages to each other.

One day he sent her a message that said, "How'd you like to go river rafting? Two buddies of mine, 'The River Rats,' need a third guide for a trip down the Salmon River next week. The guy who was supposed to go hurt his back so they have to come up with a replacement pretty quick. They asked me to fill in. It won't cost you anything."

She weighed the pros and cons. She'd never been river rafting but it was something she'd always wanted to do. It would probably be scary but she liked taking risks. Even though they hadn't traveled together before she thought they would be compatible. The work would pile up if she took time off but she had accumulated a lot of vacation time. A friend could look after her pets and plants. She couldn't think of any reason not to go.

"Yes, I'd love to go!" she responded. "Tell me what I have to do to get ready."

Packing was easy because he told her to travel light. She took a sleeping bag, an air mattress, a few clothes and toiletries, and a flashlight. He would bring a tent.

On the way, she read his guidebook and several pamphlets. She learned that the Middle Fork Salmon flows through one of the largest wilderness areas in the United States and that it offers superb class III and IV white water in a canyon of hot springs, dense forests, and sheer granite cliffs. There are niney-nine miles of magnificent river, most of it accessible only by water. "What's the meaning of these water classifications?" she asked. He replied, "The designations indicate that only experienced rafters should go down the Salmon River. But don't worry. You're in good hands. The other guides and I have spent a lot of time on this river."

When they arrived at the launch point they met the other rafters who were busily pumping up the boats. There would be twelve people on the trip. Much to her surprise, she found out she would be the only woman.

"Why didn't you tell me there wouldn't be any other women?" she asked. He tried to reassure her, saying, "I didn't know you'd be the only woman. But, believe me, it won't be a problem. You'll have a great time."

She breathed deeply, thinking, "Why didn't I ask more questions? Should I make up some kind of excuse so I don't have to go?" Another part of her said, "Enough of this ruminating. You don't want to 'chicken out' at the last minute. If you don't go you'll probably regret it."

"Come on," he said. "I'll teach you how to paddle a boat on your own so you'll begin to get the hang of it." He gave her a life jacket and wetsuit booties. He showed her how to get into a boat from the water and how to maneuver it.

Later, he demonstrated how to float in surging water. She followed him and gently merged with it. "Don't try to swim," he said. "Let the movement carry you downstream, feet first, with your knees bent." She practiced for about thirty minutes. He made the process look simple, but she knew it would take time before she could truly go with the flow.

The first day on the river was frightening and exhausting. With three boats, everyone had to paddle. The guides demonstrated a variety of strokes and how to handle the boats. The rafters climbed large waves and crashed through powerful holes. There were stretches where they drifted. But invariably, these cool, clear flows turned into narrow chutes and abrupt drops. Each time this happened her heart seemed to stop.

When they pulled over for the night she felt sore all over. Muscles that hadn't been used for a long time had been awakened. She swam in the river, changed clothes, and joined the others at the campsite.

Knowing the rafters would be ravenous, the guides prepared an abundant feast. After dinner everyone sat around the campfire and talked. One man told jokes. Another played soft melodies on a harmonica. In spite of her aching body she was glad to be part of this raft trip.

The second day on the river was even scarier than the first. The run began at a moderate tempo but it gradually built to a crescendo of tumultuous rapids until the rafters were kicking, weaving, and leaping through a narrow canyon. At times she feared for their safety. If the other rafters were afraid, they didn't let on; they seemed to be having a wonderful time. So, she kept her feelings to herself and continued paddling. She focused on trying to remember how she had been told to react, depending on the action of the water.

There was more delicious food for dinner that night. They lounged under dazzling stars and talked. She observed that the men appeared to be accepting her as a team member.

That night every muscle in her body seemed to undergo a spasm. She wondered how she'd ever get to sleep. Eventually fatigue won out and she slept soundly.

On day three she awoke with a sense of well-being. There was no pain. She had gained confidence and strength. The sense of adventure that held everyone else in its grasp had finally captured her, as well. She was eager to taste the speed and ride the tossing waves.

As they ran headlong through a series of galloping rapids of ever-escalating intensity, she whooped and screamed. The river was teeming with energy. She felt fully alive. Alternate dashes through chest-heaving rapids and canters through stretches of calm made for a perfect day.

That night they erected a huge tarp and unloaded all of the provisions. The next day was to be a day of rest. The pace was slow. Their excursion had given them a lot to talk about. They stayed up late, relishing the cool night air and the warmth of the campfire.

Their timing for erecting a tarp couldn't have been better. The next day it rained. He ventured out during a lull and caught some fish which they fried for breakfast. The tarp kept them cozy and dry. After breakfast some read, others wrote. In the afternoon the rain let up. Several of them went hiking.

That evening the guides talked to the rafters about the challenges the river had yet to offer. Soon they would be encountering a series of steep waterfalls. The most experienced guide pointed to a place on the map where it would be necessary to pull the boats over to the shore in order to scout the falls. Although The River Rats had navigated this river before, the conditions of the river could change radically depending on the rainfall. They wanted to get all the information they could about the current situation before taking it on.

Sheer heart-thumping excitement was palpable on the fifth day. Anticipating what lay ahead, everyone was eager to get an early start. The river was more challenging than ever. But by now they'd developed tight teamwork and could engage in well-coordinated, split-second maneuvers.

The first sign that anything significantly different was going to happen came from the sound. It began as a dull, but unmistakable, roar. Gradually, it got louder. Then the thunder of the falls reverberated through the canyon like the sound of a hundred horses galloping by. They pulled over, secured the boats, and hiked up the canyon wall to take a look.

The waterfalls were awesome. Here the river bulged, flexed, then exploded into gnashing, foam-filled eruptions of white water. The steep, convoluted gorge was lined with smooth white granite boulders. How would it be possible for the rubber boats to make it through such a frenzy of crashing waves?

The guides conferred for about half an hour. Finally, they agreed on a plan which they shared with the group. Each person was assigned a specific position based on physical strength. The guides went over the instructions several times so everyone would know what to do. Above all, no one must panic. They said, "If you start feeling panicky, be sure to keep paddling. Everyone has to continue to paddle in order to maintain balance."

The boat with the most experienced guide went first. The other two boats followed, mirroring each movement of the lead boat. The run bucked and throbbed like an unbroken stallion. Suddenly they were in a steep drop of incredible turbulence. They flashed and danced through a multitude of rapids, each more cataclysmic than the one before. Here was the ultimate challenge of their trip—the action-packed, rip-roaring run the earlier part of the river had prepared them for.

Just as they were entering the last set of rapids, a gigantic wall of water hit her from the side. Instantly, she was swept out of the boat into a swirling vortex. Before she could position her body to float on the surface of the river, she was pulled under. Had she not looked up at the very moment someone pushed a paddle down far enough for her to grab it, she would have drowned.

She didn't remember much about what happened after that. Apparently, the rafters in the boat behind hers pulled her out of the water and did what they could to calm her down. They took turns watching her because she was in such a severe state of shock, she didn't respond when they spoke to her.

Finally, they reached a wide, open area of lush foliage. Everyone breathed a sigh of relief. Somehow she got out of her wet clothes and into her sleeping bag. Although he felt bad that she'd fallen out of the boat, he couldn't think of anything to say. Nor could any of the others. There was no campfire that night. No one was in a talkative mood.

More churning water and some low waterfalls greeted them on the seventh day. By now, the rafters were skilled enough to handle the boats without assistance. It was time for the guides to kick back and enjoy the ride.

The day was spent jetting down a succession of rollicking rapids and meandering through soothing calms. By late afternoon they came upon a beach and a dock that was owned by a couple who maintained what had to be one of the most remote snack bars in the country. The rafters indulged in hamburgers, french fries, and ice cold beer, thanks to one of the guides who'd had enough foresight to bring along some cash.

Then they paddled through more pounding, raft-tossing white water interspersed with long, warm pools that were perfect for swimming. High points included seeing mountain sheep, bathing in a hot springs, and finding a natural slide from a high rock to a deep, gurgling pool.

When they reached the end of their journey they were greeted by the family of one of the rafters. His wife had driven their camping trailer down to the riverside. There was a huge washtub full of cold beer and a picnic supper.

The rafters were in a pensive mood. They talked about what the trip meant to each of them. One man raved about the exhilaration of the speed and big waves. Another told how the experience had led to some serious rethinking about his career. A third said the trip had whetted his appetite for seeing other wild places. Toasting the guides and each other, they agreed they'd had a terrific time. No one said a word about the fact that she had nearly drowned.

The rafters departed as each of their rides showed up to drive them back to the point of origin. Finally, he and she were the only ones left waiting.

It began to get dark; the air got cool. She built a fire and changed into dry clothes. Should they put up the tent? Where on earth was their ride? They had a canteen of water and a little food but not enough to sustain them for very long. He had a map so they knew where they were. But that wasn't much help. All it showed was that they were in an extremely isolated spot without a telephone, provisions, or transportation.

The more she thought about the circumstances, the more prayers she uttered silently. "Dear God," she pleaded, "Never again will I get into trouble as a result of not knowing how to assert myself. If you let me get out of this situation alive, I promise I will bend over backwards to ask questions. Instead of trying to pretend I am relaxed and easy-going when I am anxious, I will be direct and matter-of-fact. I also pledge I won't allow my life to get so boring that I take foolhardy risks."

Finally, at 2 a.m., a noisy RV arrived on the scene. It was their ride back to the point of origin. The driver apologized. The fan belt had broken and he didn't have a spare. It had taken him eight hours to hitch a ride to a gas station, buy a new belt, get a ride back to the van, and reach the rendezvous site.

7. The Mosaic

Magical Mystery Mime Troupe and Jazz Band

I'm what you'd call an average sort of person. I work hard and try to do a good job. I don't have any musical talent or acting ability and have never longed for any. Sure, I like to go to movies occasionally but I prefer reading murder mysteries or watching "whodunits" on TV.

In spite of all this, I keep having the craziest dream! The first time this happened was about three years ago. After the second time I began writing down what I could remember when I woke up. Then I got to where I would wake up right after the dream. This way I could record more of the details. Although it has never become a full blown nightmare, sometimes I awaken with an empty sensation in the pit of my stomach, kind of like what happens when you ride a rollercoaster.

The dream goes like this . . . I am part of a caravan with this traveling group of performers. We do a combination of street theater, circus, and musical review. All the acts are improvisational so we never know what we'll be doing until we're actually doing it. Once I caught a glimpse of the opening of our tent. Balloons and ribbons were strung along the top. A colorful banner announced "The Magical Mystery Mime Troupe and Jazz Band."

If you knew me, you would realize this is a pretty strange dream. For one thing, I have a very secure job and enjoy the people I work with. Second, I'm a workaholic. It's hard for me to tear myself away because I'm so committed to my work.

And as for the idea of improvisation . . . forget it. I'm a very careful planner. I was taught to plan my work and work my plan. I *never* do anything on impulse and I think people who do are usually sorry.

But the weirdest part of all, as far as I'm concerned, is the reason why this mime troupe exists. It seems we have all come together to create an interactive blend of theater and music in order to generate audience collaboration. We invite the audience to join us in creating a communal, artistic experience. Everyone becomes a star.

Now, I have to tell you that not by the wildest stretch of imagination would my friends and colleagues associate me with communal anything. By nature I'm a loner. Naturally, at work I do my bit as a team player. But during the little free time there is, I prefer my own company. I choose to live alone, travel alone, eat alone, and take responsibility for myself.

The reason I'm telling you all this is to show you just how bizarre dreams can be and how troublesome it was for me to have this dream keep coming back to haunt me. Also, I think it's important that you know a little bit about me so you can fully appreciate how shocked I was when strange things began happening in my real life.

The first thing I recall that was out of the ordinary took place when I was having lunch with two associates about a year ago. We agreed to meet to talk about an important project. After we finished discussing business matters one of them asked, "If you could quit your job tomorrow and do anything you wanted, what would you choose to do?" Without a moment's hesitation Elise blurted out, "Oh, I know exactly what I'd do! I'd go to clown school in Florida then I'd join a traveling circus. Since I was little I've always dreamed about dressing up in funny clothes and making people laugh."

As she said these words, I experienced a tingling sensation in my body and the hair on the back of my neck felt like it was standing straight up. Imagine my shock when Celeste chimed in, "I think that sounds wonderful! Since I was six years old I have wanted to have a huge wardrobe so I could dress up and pretend I'm on stage. I'd like nothing better than to travel all over the world, eat exotic food, and meet lots of interesting people."

When they turned to me all I could think of was my recurring dream. Should I tell them? "No," a firm voice said inside me. "You don't know them well enough to share something as personal as a dream." So I simply said, "I'm quite satisfied with the way things are. I don't want to quit my job or go anywhere else." But this incident had a profound effect on me. I couldn't stop thinking about how odd it was that I was dreaming their dream.

That night both Elise and Celeste appeared in my dream. Celeste and I were inside a small church. Along with everyone else we were singing, moving, and shouting, "Amen!" We were there because she thought it was a good way for us to connect with the people in that community. Elise was wearing an elegant leather outfit with high boots. She was driving a large van that seemed to serve as our living quarters, except as I watched her navigate the turns, the van changed into a horse-drawn cart and she was going on and on about the need to take care of her horses.

The next day I was in a bookstore looking for a good murder mystery. It occurred to me there might be a book on interpreting dreams. I found a small book with summaries of a number of themes. The author said, "Dreams can serve as a path to the sacred world of your inner self. They may point to problem areas that keep you stuck. They may also open doors to creativity, emotional healing, and spiritual growth."[3]

I looked up the word, "journey." All it said was, " . . . your own journey through life." There were references to obstacles, destinations, different vehicles, and collisions, but none of these had appeared in my dreams so far. The only reference to "church" was "buildings." There was no listing for "van." For "car" and "cart" it said, "This image may capture your desire to get away, leave home, or move on." The reference for "horse" said, "This symbol may refer to unconscious energy, which you are preparing to use."

Now I was more puzzled than ever. Was it possible that at some unconscious level I wanted to get away or move on? I dismissed the part about the horses. Elise has a horse ranch on ten acres of rolling hills and she loves to ride. It was natural for her to be connected with horses in the dream.

The next unnerving event happened about a month after the lunch meeting. I got a call from Elise inviting me to her place for dinner on a

Sunday evening. As I said, I value privacy and am accustomed to keeping to myself on weekends. Nevertheless, Celeste would be there and I like both of them so I accepted the invitation.

Elise has a warm, welcoming way about her which makes her a good hostess. Her home mirrors her personality. Over the years she has bought antique furniture, oriental rugs, colorful vases, and things that give her home a cozy air. We sat on the large veranda overlooking the creek and woods, drinking in the scenery along with our wine.

Elise also invited another friend who was a cabaret singer named Sabrina. Everything about Sabrina was dramatic . . . her clothes, her physical features, her way of speaking, and her approach to life. She offered to do a Tarot reading for each of us.

Somehow I was selected to go first. In my reading I got the Moon card. Sabrina explained, "In the Tarot tradition the Moon represents unconscious desires. The Moon is also a symbol for the fear of losing control or falling into the unconscious realm of sleep and dreams. This card is calling you to enter the darkness and make a journey into a labyrinth. If you're afraid to enter your own astral territory you will never truly know yourself. If you can surrender to the darkness your journey will be full of revelation."

I felt the blood drain from my face. A wooziness came over me. Was I going to faint? By the look on my face they all knew I was seriously affected by the reading. Sabrina leaned toward me and asked, "Are you all right? You look like you've seen a ghost."

I have never taken much of an interest in dreams or mystical stuff but I felt I was being drawn into the darkness. Obviously, Sabrina knew more about this path than I so I made a hasty decision to trust her guidance. I hoped Elise and Celeste would keep my confession confidential.

Sharing my dreams broke the ice. Sabrina was supportive and reassuring. She loaned me two books she thought would be helpful and encouraged me to call her whenever I wished. We spent the rest of the evening telling jokes and laughing. We sang songs and told stories about our childhood. I left feeling deeply moved by the way we were able to be direct and honest with each other and by the fun we'd shared.

The following week I was surprised to discover that, by sharing my dreams and permitting myself to be vulnerable, I had become stronger. And, by letting down a few of my self-imposed barriers, I had gained an increased sense of security.

In the months to come the four of us got together frequently. Sometimes we invited others to join us in reading plays, poems, and short stories aloud. Near the end of each gathering everyone would make suggestions for the location and theme of the next event. A decision would be made by general agreement. We didn't do a lot of planning because no one wanted to interfere with the spontaneity.

For a Halloween party we wore costumes showing sides of ourselves that were seldom seen. Deciding to shed my usual image, I went as a court jester. It took a month to make my costume and learn to juggle but I enjoyed every minute of it.

Midway through the party we exchanged costumes so each of us could experiment with different roles. All evening Sabrina had been gushing over my costume. When it was her turn to try it on she beamed. She didn't want to take it off. I told her to wear the costume home and return it to me later.

That night I did something I rarely do: I read my horoscope in the newspaper. My astrological sign is Cancer. The person who writes this column has the same sign. The reading said, "I'm not a wanderer or a clown, but I've been dreaming I am. So believe me, I know wanderers and clowns when I see them. And right now you are radiating the pure essence of a wanderer and clown."[4]

I was surprised to find how much I looked forward to our get-togethers. We talked about all sorts of things, from complex issues such as freedom and death, to pithy subjects like what went into a delicious casserole we were eating.

The only problem was that during the process of becoming a member of this small community I gradually got to a point where I was relinquishing too much. I found myself going out of my way to make certain others' needs were met. I stopped taking issue with ideas that were different from mine. And I developed a habit of agreeing to do whatever others asked even when their requests inconvenienced me a great deal.

I noticed that, without discussing it, some people in the group adopted an attitude of "What's yours is mine." Take Sabrina, for example. She never returned my court jester costume. I didn't want to bring up the subject because it seemed trivial but it did bother me.

And then there was the nagging thing about Peter. He was a friend of Elise's who had become a regular member of our group. A couple of times I brought friends of mine to our gatherings. Peter didn't say anything to me, directly, but he told Elise that he thought this jeopardized the camaraderie we'd developed. She passed his objections on to me. Not wanting to offend Peter, I stopped inviting outsiders. Still, I wish he'd talked to me about his point of view.

My travel dream continued and kept me on the road with a group of people. In one episode we were sitting in a circle playing a game. I didn't know what game it was but I understood the rules. We were laughing and having a good time. Suddenly, the game changed and I no longer knew the rules. It involved a deck of cards I had never seen before. Although they joked about it, the others said I couldn't play. I awoke with a feeling of emptiness in my stomach.

The next morning I looked up "game" in my dream dictionary. It said, "You may be trying to look at the conflicts of life as a game, possibly indicating a deep desire to make light of something serious." The reference to "card games" said, "This image can throw light on your current conflict. For example, it may indicate that your success depends on developing strategies and tactics with the cards you have, rather than relying on getting new cards."

In winter the flu hit hard. I was in bed for eight days. During this time the members of our group were like family to me. They brought food and made sure I ate it. They called to check on my progress and see if I needed anything. Elise sent flowers. Celeste circulated a terrific get-well card. As soon as I felt well enough to sit up and read they gave me several murder mysteries.

I also read a book about how Martin Buber looked at relationships. He said the essence of community is "the center," which is made up of relationships people hold in common that override all other relationships they have in their lives.

Lying in bed gave me lots of time to think. I couldn't help speculating about my life. Without being aware of it I had become part of a caring community. The border between myself and other people had eased.

For the most part I felt good about how I was getting connected to other people. There was one drawback, however. The relationships I held in common with my friends had overridden my relationship with myself.

When Sabrina came to visit I told her of my concern. She gave me a book about myths, art, and Tarot that described the role of a shaman. It said the objective of a shaman's journeys is to heal the physical body and the human spirit, both of individuals and the community at large.

Taking a step toward healing my spirit, I enrolled in an introductory improvisation class. I thought giving myself a gift would help me get back to being a friend to myself.

I had so much fun in the beginning class that I signed up for advanced training. Midway through this class our coach invited us to accompany her to a session she was offering inside a maximum security prison.

Now I go once a week to take part in an improv experience at the prison. As a result of our shared values and purpose, frequent interaction, and the rapport we've developed, the members of our group have become committed to each other in ways that go beyond the formal sessions. We are in touch with each other regularly and can confide our innermost thoughts without fear of judgment, ridicule, or unsolicited advice. We're experiencing what it's like to be living in community even though some members of our group live behind bars.

In my most recent travel dream people were moving to the rhythm of a jazz band. Everyone was in a festive mood. Our costumes were consistent with the theme that life is a circus. In the dream I remember thinking how clear our purpose had become. It was to bind us together in community through a shared experience that all of us would enjoy.

8. The Sphere

Dance with Gaia

I'd like to welcome all of you who are here to learn about our trips to the moon. I love sharing our experiences! It's hard to believe that I, Marin Matthews, have gone to the moon and back three times.

One reason I make these presentations is I want to share the gift of space travel. Seeing the Earth from space was only a conceptual notion not too long ago. Now it's a visual reality.

What you are about to see are films from our missions. Although you won't be able to experience directly what we saw, you will witness just how breathtakingly beautiful the Earth is from space.

I also want to convey how travel into space has made me aware of the Earth as a system. I hope that my words, combined with pictures from space, will give you a sense of our planet as a living organism.

Once you're in space it doesn't take long before you realize that everyone and everything on the Earth is interdependent. During our first day in space we pointed out nations; then we identified continents. By the time we reached the moon, however, the entire Earth was the focus of our attention. At that distance we could see how everything is connected. Borders that have been erected for political and economic reasons don't exist when you get that far away.

A few words about myself . . . I was raised in Dayton, Ohio, home of the Wright brothers. Growing up, I thought I could do anything I set my mind to if I was willing to work hard enough. My parents never forced me into any pattern nor did they tell me that because I was a girl I had to do things a certain way. I was always curious and wanted to do new things, see new places, and meet new people.

It was only natural that I would want to be an explorer because both of my parents followed this path. My mother explored inner space as a Jungian therapist. My father was a test pilot who developed a business building small aircraft.

From the time I was little I can remember flying with my mom and dad to attend air shows and visit friends who were just as crazy about flying machines as my dad. He was the one who taught me how to fly when I was thirteen years old.

Even in my dreams I flew. Sometimes I woke up disappointed because I couldn't really fly on my own. I used to hike way up in the hills above our house to be with the birds. I spent hours watching them soar.

When I was seventeen I met a man at an air show who lived in the Mohave Desert. He was building a rocket in his backyard (an area that covered 1500 acres.) We talked for a long time. As we parted, he invited me to come to California to see his operation.

I saved enough money from my part-time job as a flight mechanic to visit him during summer vacation. A friend agreed to give me a lift in her private plane.

I had a terrific time getting to know this aerospace entrepreneur! I learned about space shuttles, rockets, and moonwalks. He told me as soon as he achieved the necessary reliability of his rocket, he would launch it with an astronaut on board. He wanted to demonstrate the viability of an alternative to government-sponsored space programs and was trying to raise money from private sources. The first flight would be just a "suborbital dash into space," as he put it. Nothing complicated would be needed in terms of a life support system. "You could practically hold your breath that long," he said, halfway in jest.

From that moment on, I knew I wanted to be an astronaut. I made up my mind I would be the one to make the first flight for this noble endeavor, helping to create more opportunities for others to get involved in space travel.

The demonstration flight took place three years later. It was a joint venture on the part of American and Russian scientists and engineers who wanted to turn space missions into a profitable industry. The flight was an engineering and commercial success. It attracted the attention of over a dozen corporate executives around the world who recognized the potential for new business. Each contributed a sizable investment toward creating an international consortium that would send three astronauts to the moon. I knew I wanted to be a member of that team.

Seven years later the consortium sent a spacecraft to the moon. The first in a series of trips aimed at building a small research and development colony, this mission lasted a month. I was one of the astronauts on this mission.

Nothing I ever read of the accounts of space travel came close to preparing me for the total impact of this journey. For example, I knew what weightlessness would feel like; my training had prepared me for that. But I had never been weightless for such a prolonged period of time.

Being weightless means you completely lose your grounding. The thing you're used to pushing back on and having remain stable is gravity. Normally, you just let gravity take over—you sink into a chair or fall into bed. But when you're weightless, nothing takes over. There is no pull. In weightlessness it's as though you no longer have a body. You aren't connected to anything, physically, except the clothes and spacesuit you're wearing.

So, I wasn't completely prepared for weightlessness. Nor was I fully prepared for what happened when I first left the spacecraft to walk on the moon's surface. It was very hard to cope with the glistening blackness and incomprehensible emptiness of space. Knowing there could be a malfunction and I might not come back to the Earth was a sobering thought. I recalled the scene in *2001: A Space Odyssey* where the HAL 9000 computer cut the astronaut loose and he went floating into stark black infinity.

It took until the end of the first week before I began to feel comfortable walking on the surface of the moon. The tension eased as I became more and more captivated by the sight of the Earth. Working with my partner, we agreed to cover for each other so we could steal glances in the direction of home and fully experience what a gorgeous gem our planet is. Her sheer beauty made me catch my breath. I remember thinking, "This is the most perfect creation one could ever imagine!"

What was happening to us has happened to other astronauts. Even though the purpose of the space program is to explore new worlds, for many of us it produces an even more astounding discovery—the Earth. Many years ago Norman Cousins noted that setting eyes on the Earth was even more significant for the Apollo astronauts than setting foot on the moon.

A fellow astronaut once joked about how the Earth should be called "Water," since it makes up seven tenths of the Earth's surface. Predominantly blue, our planet dances in a black sea of space. The amount and intensity of blue is difficult to describe. In 1990, Voyager 2 turned its cameras back toward the Earth from a distance of 3.7 billion miles and radioed back the images. Even from the frontiers of the solar system the Earth could be seen as a pale, blue dot.

In the space shuttle we moved at a speed of 17,000 miles per hour. At this speed the scenery constantly shifts. No view of the Earth is ever the same. Nature, itself, is alive.

On the ground we're used to seeing lightning as harsh, sudden, and localized during rainstorms. From the vantage point of an astronaut, however, lightning is a global event. One flash of light can be seen halfway around the Earth. Like a bolt from the fingertips of Zeus, lightening ripples and cracks, even though the sound is inaudible at that distance. Witnessing this energy in nature gave us a feeling of strength. It seemed like we could reach out and tap into the power of the planet.

In space my partners and I were struck by the extent to which we could appreciate the cycle of life and death on the Earth. From this vantage point nothing ever really dies. Death means becoming part of another living subsystem. The ground on which we walk is made up of the dust of our ancestors. Our own bodies will return to the ground to feed the trees and plants, which will nurture future human beings.

As we began to accept that life has a spaciousness greater than our own, time took on an altogether different meaning. The whole point of life became being fully aware of what was happening in the present. "Now" became enormous; it expanded to fill up all of our senses. There was no past and no future, separate from the present.

We became aware of the life force in everything. Even killing ants was something we talked about. Now don't get me wrong; I'm not saying that killing ants is the same as killing people. What I am suggesting is that we should be less eager to kill anything that might temporarily annoy us. And we should stop killing people as though they were ants!

A recurring topic of discussion was, what if there are higher forms of life to which we humans are related, much like individual cells are related to our entire bodies? A cell has a limited ability to appreciate reality beyond a certain point. Perhaps our supreme arrogance is in thinking we make up the superior form of life.

After I came back and tried to pick up my life where I'd left off, I found that planning for the short term seemed narrow-minded and pointless. I decided to take an active role in promoting a long-term view of the Earth as a place to cherish, restore, and sustain. Once my mission was the moon. Now I am a Friend of Gaia.

Thus far in the life of humankind Mother Earth has continued to nourish us, while healing all the wounds we've inflicted on her. This self-regulating ability is what James Lovelock calls, "The Gaia Hypothesis." As an authority on the biosphere, he postulates that the system consisting of the exposed continents, the oceans, and the atmosphere has been balanced for millions of years. By controlling the chemical and physical environment, the biosphere maintains stability and keeps our planet healthy.

But what we call evolution has been, in many respects, a demolition. Most of us were taught to think in terms of having dominion over the Earth. This position has put the fragile gem at our mercy. Through the space program we have amassed an awesome collection of pictures of the Earth. Many of these photographs provide concrete evidence that the health of our planet is at risk.

We can only see so far when we look up into the sky and we have trouble imagining what we can't directly experience. Consequently, we take the Earth's atmosphere for granted. It looks pretty deep from where we stand. But this is an illusion. In reality, the atmosphere is like a fragile ribbon that has seen a lot of wear and tear. It is frayed. There are signs of holes. One astronaut remarked how he had thought of the atmosphere as the skin of an orange until he saw the Earth from space. After seeing the results of pollution, he said the atmosphere is much more like the delicate skin of an onion.

My purpose is to convey the importance supporting Gaia's return to a healthy state. Joining in the dance means pursuing an Earth-based spirituality in which we understand we are all cells in the body of Gaia. The dance calls for us to look at the Earth from her point of view as well as our own. And it requires us to maintain a natural balance with the land so we can sustain it for the generations to come.

The Aborigines in Australia have always assumed that everything on the planet is interdependent. Throughout history they have methodically asked this question in regard to everything they do, "Is this in the highest good for all life everywhere?" This question is at the heart of what it means to be a Friend of Gaia.

In summary, there are five basic steps for the dance with Gaia. They are:

1. *Appreciate that everything on the Earth is alive.* Regard all life as sacred.
2. *Accept that everyone and everything is connected.* Find ways to live so you are close to the land. Establish ties with people around the world.

3. *Remember that energy flows where your attention goes.* Make an effort to be fully conscious of possible ramifications of your actions. Be aware of how you act to set in motion any series of changes in form, such as through killing or destroying anything. Abide by the Native American tradition of thinking of what you do from the standpoint of its potential effects on children who will be born seven generations from now.

4. *Act with personal integrity.* Take responsibility for what is happening on the planet. Practice stewardship in place of ownership. Make it a practice to give something back.

5. *Use the beauty in nature as a source of energy and inspiration.* Tap your own wellspring of vision and intuition to regenerate the social order. In the company of others, aspire to accomplish extraordinary things.

After the film presentation, I will be happy to answer any questions you may have.

PART THREE

Creating New Realities

The most astounding example of the way that we allow bureaucracies to control our lives is our commitment to the idea that the economic system must "help" people by "providing jobs.". . . In a surplus economy, the idea that we must provide jobs for people forces us to promote economic growth, even if most of the products we produce are useless . . . We lose sight of the fact that we are actually demanding to do unnecessary work.

> CHARLES SIEGEL
> "A New Declaration of Independence"

Daily habit and what has been done in the past . . . are forms. We can draw intelligently from these forms, yet we must not forget the other side—the absolute formless which has never been limited. Inevitably, as we bring the formless into our consciousness our human nervous system will form it and limit it. The challenge is to play on the edge—the edge of the unformed.

> BROOKE MEDICINE EAGLE
> in Shape Shifters: Shaman Women in
> Contemporary Society

In work do what you enjoy.

> LAO-TZU
> Tao Te Ching

9. The House of Elan

Sunny's Place in the Circle

Sunny initiated a series of storytelling seminars to help people make sense of what happens in organizational systems. Her approach enabled the participants to identify different kinds of organizations, predict what does and does not work within each of them, and become aware of alternatives.

Recent graduates found the material useful in choosing jobs and understanding their organizations once they were hired. Seasoned employees used the ideas to discern what makes an organization wholesome so they could locate healthier environments. Those who felt like misfits applied the approach to find employment where there was a better match for their personalities and skills. People who were suffering from work-related stress experienced relief by learning how to find jobs in work settings that fostered harmony rather than discord.

But some of the participants reported that the descriptive account fell short of meeting their needs and expectations. In addition to learning how to understand organizational systems, these people wanted to take action. Some wanted to change their organizations; others were seeking guidance in creating something entirely new.

After giving these requests a great deal of thought, Sunny awoke one morning to the sound of the Old Woman's voice. "It's time for you to awaken the shaman within by acknowledging your greater purpose in life," the voice said. "Accept your place in the circle. Help people regain their power. Show them how to bring about social and economic change."

Sunny accepted her place in the circle by beginning to write her own story as she wanted it to read. She asked herself, "What makes up my emotional acre?" "What do I care enough about to defend against intrusion?" "How do I fit into the grand scheme of things?" "What kinds of work can I do that are fun and exciting?" "How can I live so I feel vibrant and alive every day?"

It took several weeks to answer these questions to her satisfaction. Eventually, her effort was rewarded. She decided that what she wanted to do more than anything else was to start a nontraditional business and educational venture based on the following conditions:

- It would channel her needs, interests, and talents.
- It would provide opportunities to exercise all five shapes and make her more flexible and resilient.
- It would draw on strengths from all five realities.
- It would support diversity and innovation.
- It would be designed to eliminate routine conflicts and would incorporate rituals aimed at resolving disagreements.
- It would integrate work with the rest of her life.

By getting clear about what she wanted she gained energy and felt inspired. She was excited by the prospect of creating a style of life that far surpassed what she had envisioned at the beginning of her search for alternatives to the sandboxes.

Her ability to assume five shapes could be put to use right away. Her skills as an Organizer would enable her to construct a firm structure. She would draw on her capacity as a Strategist as she adopted a project orientation, developed a crisp game plan, and introduced productive processes. She would tap her Communicator capacity as she connected with new people, learned from others, engaged in dialogue, and exchanged ideas. Her prior experiences in serving as a Bridge would empower her to build a community composed of people, ideas, and resources. Her Friend of Gaia attributes would be utilized as she planted seeds of ideas to foster the development of a healthy organization.

A Shamanic Community

Sunny knew her project was far too big to develop by herself. She needed the collective strength of a group. So, she initiated a search for people who shared her interests and who would pool their power and influence to accomplish things they could not do alone.

As she discussed her ideas with colleagues and friends, they helped her get clear about the kinds of people she was seeking. Finally, she completed her wish list. She would look for partners with the potential to become contemporary shamans. As healers, visionaries, adventurers, guides, power brokers, and peacemakers, they would possess these characteristics:

- *Mind:* They would be pragmatists with experience in all five organizational systems. They would want to use their knowledge and expertise to develop a successful, nontraditional business and educational venture. They would know how to use altered states to push on to new directions. They would be willing to risk and eager to learn.

• *Body:* They would be "flexers"—people interested in becoming more resilient. They would acknowledge the importance of natural foods to a healthful style of life. They would regard forms of self-expression such as storytelling, singing, and dancing as essential to physical well-being.

• *Soul:* They would be willing to invest emotionally in a project aimed at healing and creating. From deep within the centers of their being they would be able to tap a wellspring of vision, integrity, and intuition.

• *Spirit:* They would accept the principle that everything is energy and that all forms of life are sacred. They would understand how to stay in touch with their higher selves. They would be open to guidance by divine inspiration and would find joy in inspiring others.

She sent out flyers and arranged for radio announcements. A notice that she placed in a daily newspaper said:

Cooperation is important both at home and in the workplace. Help build a more humane world by becoming part of a cohousing community where your work is integrated with the rest of your life. I am looking for partners in a non-traditional business/educational venture aimed at developing wholesome organizations.

After receiving a deluge of responses, she scheduled several public meetings to present her ideas. At these meetings she explained how she wanted to use the positive aspects of five ways to live and work to create a sixth path. She discussed her wish list for partners and answered as many questions as she could.

Eventually, she found five individuals who shared her vision. This core group began meeting to form a plan of action. They studied the five realities, assessed their ability to change shape, and composed their own life stories.

Then they exchanged ideas about the lives they would love to live. Among the things all of them liked to do were cooking, eating good food, and engaging in stimulating conversation. They were elated to discover that four of them were recipe collectors, three had small gardens, one was a tinkerer who invented kitchen gadgets, and one was compiling an online cookbook for cats.

What kind of an enterprise would offer something for gourmet chefs, gadget aficionados, recipe exchangers, gardeners, and people who enjoy getting together to talk? They brainstormed, wrote short stories, drew pictures, and performed skits until they came up with an original concept. They resolved to open an establishment devoted to nourishing the mind, body, and spirit. Dealing in food preparation, it would also serve as an educational institute and a center for renewal. The clientele would include customers who appreciate good food, people who enjoy sharing food for thought, and those interested in learning about the processes the partners were using to make their dream a reality.

The partners came to an agreement regarding their purpose. It would be:

- to lead a satisfying life;
- to promote organizational change;
- to provide excellent products and services;
- to create an environment conducive to learning; and
- to make a profit.

After discussing what it would take to be successful, the partners compiled a list of specifications. They concurred that their enterprise would boast wise and humane management, be fiscally sound, and have a social conscience. The decision making process would be democratic: one person, one vote. Decisions would be made on the basis of a two-thirds majority opinion. Additional elements they identified as critical to their success included the following:

- a large enough group to organize the common activities over a period of many years;
- a structure that would foster harmony, openness, and tolerance;
- guiding principles to support their purpose;
- clear goals and realistic expectations;
- access to external sources of replentishment;
- effective ways to solicit suggestions for improvement;
- functional boundaries, such as protection in their personal lives from the demands of the enterprise;
- flexible work arrangements;
- procedures to support the free expression of feelings;
- avenues for realistic and honest feedback; and nonblaming modes of expression;
- acceptance of conflict when it plays a productive role, such as a signaling a need for change or serving as a spark for innovation;
- rituals for managing differences, such as sounding boards to address problems, dialogues to explore diversity, and rules for fair fighting;
- routines to avoid domination by people with strong personalities;
- forums to talk about pressures and to promote the sharing of responsibilities;
- symbolic milestones and celebrations to mark the achievement of significant goals;
- a place that, when people come to work, they don't wish they were somewhere else;

• activities to engender community; and
• balance between a marketplace orientation and the spiritual aspects of work.

It took the partners three years to make their dream a reality. During this period they made field trips to cohousing communities and talked with people who were experimenting with other kinds of lifestyles. They spent an enormous amount of time conducting research, convening meetings, and making decisions.

Learning how to make decisions as a group was not easy. They had to develop cohesion and acquire group interaction skills. As they worked together to address their needs and wants they found out that they didn't have to agree to get along nor did they have to get along to agree.

Once they had enough of a plan to get started, they combined their financial resources and purchased a large piece of property located just outside a metropolitan area. The parcel was big enough to accommodate fifteen separate residences, a community center, and the building that would house their business and educational venture.

To reduce costs, they did the landscaping and part of the interior construction themselves. Some projects were fun; others were just hard work. They learned not to get burned out on the latter.

At the point when most of the construction was completed, they held a celebration and named their community and their enterprise. Because the project grew out of their collective imaginations, captured their enthusiasm for food, gave them renewed vigor, and was created with flair, they used the French word, *élan*. They named their group "The Elan Community," their business venture "The House of Elan," and their educational project "The Elan Institute."Within their community all of the homes were designed and built by the partners, who occupied six of the dwellings. Friends and family members purchased the other nine homes.

The community center featured a large, well-equipped kitchen and a dining room to seat all of the members. (The residences were equipped with self-sufficient kitchens so people could eat meals in their homes if they chose.) The center was designed to house a children's playroom, a child care facility, a game room, a dark room for photography, study rooms, workshops, guest rooms, storage compartments for tools and bicycles, and a laundry. Tennis courts, a playground, and a swimming pool were located outside the community center.

The Best of Five Worlds

To ensure the creation of a wholesome system, the partners identified the strengths in each of Sunny's short stories. Then they made a conscious effort to incorporate strengths from all five stories in their community, their business enterprise, and their educational institute. The following description summarizes the results of this endeavor.

Strengths Drawn from "King Of The Mountain":

The House of Elan has an identifiable structure and is well organized. The partners prepare budgets, formulate policies, compile schedules, operate according to specific procedures, and keep records of all transactions. They acknowledge the importance of details, form, and order. People who work in the records department on the first floor conduct research concerning lifestyles of the free and joyful.The enterprise is enriched through meaningful rituals. The partners regularly convene forums, meetings, and celebrations.

Strengths Drawn from "Motocross":

The partners are pragmatic, efficient, and financially astute. They generate sales strategies and devise new products. They appreciate the importance of steadily increasing their profits, maintaining a competitive edge, and gradually expanding the business. By successfully marketing to people in lucrative niches, they frequently surpass their established goals and objectives.

Strengths Drawn from "White Water Rafting":

Principles of self-management are used. Salaries and work schedules are set by the partners and employee benefits are self-selected. The business meetings are open to all. Customers participate in decision making and problem solving. The Elan Institute is dedicated to lifelong learning. The partners constantly expand their skills through rotation and cross-training.

Communication is facilitated through videos and a newsletter. The third floor computer network links The House of Elan with customers, recipients of services, and other enterprises. To ensure continuous improvement, the partners encourage feedback from customers through an electronic bulletin board, attendance at meetings, and a suggestion box. Word-of-mouth advertising plays a crucial role in the success of their business. At least half of the customers come to The House of Elan because their friends recommend it.

Strengths Drawn from "Magical Mystery Mime Troupe and Jazz Band":

The partners choose to live and work together in a small community. The community charter articulates a purpose based on shared ideals, values, and beliefs. Mutual respect prevails.

Throughout the community there is a both-and focus. An emphasis on individual rights is balanced with attention to shared responsibilities. The physical layout addresses both the need of the community for socializing and the need for privacy on the part of individuals. Life and work are integrated.

There is a rich social atmosphere. The landscape design encourages interaction and increases the possibility of face-to-face contact.

At bi-monthly community meetings members catch up on news, discuss issues, and make decisions. Once a year there is a community-wide evaluation. During this period the community members go beyond discussing routine business issues and explore how to make things better. They note concerns and agree on action plans. After the evaluation period they have a big community festival.

The business is community-owned and operated. Everyone is rewarded for success. All of the community members own stock and share the profits. The division of labor is equitable. The community members share meal preparation, domestic chores, and child care.

The partners believe good business and a social conscience go hand in hand, so they give something back to the larger community of which they are a part. They participate in local events and provide training opportunities for young people. Ten percent of the earnings from The House of Elan goes to nonprofit groups.

Strengths Drawn from "Dance With Gaia":

The partners maintain both a short-term and a long-term view. They look forward to establishing a second location abroad. This will provide an opportunity to increase their connection with others around the world.

The House of Elan is founded on life-serving principles. The partners ensure that their business grows naturally. It changes as they change. The enterprise is organic. The partners avoid using pesticides and they employ natural ingredients in their products whenever possible.

The Community of Elan utilizes renewable energy sources. The community building has 1800 square feet of solar panels on the roof which furnish power for radiant space heating and domestic hot water. A windmill generates electricity.

To use as little land as possible the partners built a five-story commercial building and houses that have two stories. All of the buildings are constructed to conserve heat. They feature concrete slab floors, brick thermal walls, and triple glazed windows. The external wall area is minimized to make the most effective use of solar energy and to reduce temperature fluctuations.

The Ringed Pentacle

In creating a new style of life Sunny and her partners chose a symbol in place of an organizational chart to represent the structure of their project. This symbol is a ringed pentacle—a star and five circles. At each point of the star is a story, signifying a given reality. Within the circles are the individual shapes that correspond to the five realities.

As a guiding star The Ringed Pentacle serves the community well. It's an important symbol for these reasons:

- It provides an image of their whole system.
- It enables them to communicate their vision and purpose to others.
- It reminds them of their commitment to creating a style of life based on the best of five realities.
- It helps them to keep in mind the relationship between individual and organizational shapes.
- It encourages them to look at things from different points of view.

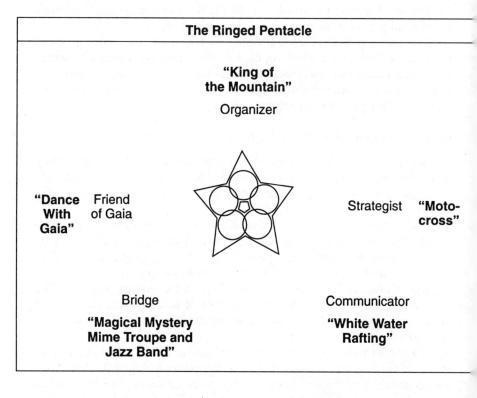

The Ringed Pentacle

"King of the Mountain"

Organizer

"Dance With Gaia"   Friend of Gaia

Strategist   **"Moto-cross"**

Bridge

"Magical Mystery Mime Troupe and Jazz Band"

Communicator

"White Water Rafting"

As the partners gave shape to their collective dream, they designed each floor of the five-story commercial building so it would represent a different reality and would provide an arena to strengthen a specific shape. Taken together, the floors form a unique whole.

Sunny is the enterprise manager and facilitator. Each partner is responsible for one floor of the business. Nevertheless, the partners cross-train each other and rotate their responsibilities so they have ample opportunity to expand their shapes.

The ground floor offers opportunities to assume the shape of an Organizer. Recipes, cookbooks, and staples are located here. A bookstore features cookbooks from around the world. Fresh herbs and exotic spices are packaged for sale in combinations based on the ethnic origins of a wide variety of recipes. All of the recipes are tested before being distributed. Chefs form a hierarchy, depending on their expertise in the culinary arts. The firm's records are housed in a separate room, along with the research division.

The second floor offers practice in assuming the shape of a Strategist. One of the things that bothered the partners was that most kitchens are laid out by people who don't cook, so this floor features two complete working kitchens. These kitchens are used to prepare all of the food that is consumed on the premises. This floor also features kitchen gadgets, cooking equipment, and electrical appliances. Experienced technicians demonstrate the importance of key processes in food preparation and how to use a variety of appliances and gadgets. Ideas concerning ways to grow the business are portrayed in colorful wall posters.

On the third floor the partners expand their capacities as Communicators. People come to this floor to trade information about food-related topics. The hub of an extensive computerized network is located here. Customers can gain access to an online gastronomic newsletter, recipe exchanges, and menus from local restaurants. There's also a network that connects people who will work for food with those who provide food in exchange for odd jobs.

The fourth floor permits the partners to gain experience in assuming the shape of a Bridge. How we relate on the basis of food is the theme of this floor. The focus is on entertaining, ambience, and food presentation. In addition to consuming delicious food in a lovely setting, people gather on the fourth floor to have fun. On weekends this floor is used for potlucks, dinner parties, jazz concerts, dances, theatrical performances, chamber music performances, storytelling sessions, songfests, and poetry readings.

The fifth floor offers opportunities to assume the shape of A Friend of Gaia. In a large roof garden the owners grow flowers, fruits, vegetables, and herbs. Soft music plays in the background. An expert is on hand to provide tips on gardening and to make seeds available. Weather permitting, the owners host gatherings to look at the night sky through telescopes.

The partners installed a circular staircase to connect the five floors so customers attracted to one floor would be inclined to explore the others, as well. Many customers have a favorite floor and are very loyal supporters of what goes on there. They argue their floor is best. Others like to browse on all of the floors.

The partners know it's important to provide an integrated, synergistic experience for their customers. Once a month they meet for dinner on the fourth floor. Using the stage to act out their dreams, desires, and fantasies, they explore new ways to connect the offerings and activities on all five floors.

The House of Elan has developed a reputation for being a center for the unexpected. Even though they come for many different reasons, most people discover something new. Someone who wants to purchase a recipe book ends up getting linked to the online newsletter. A person who comes to eat good food also makes new friends. An individual who uses the roof garden as a source of fresh fruits and vegetables rekindles a fascination for tinkering with gadgets.

10. A Life Changing Approach

Through The Elan Institute Sunny and her partners show people how to use their collective power to change organizations and follow their chosen paths. The partners work with networks of people inside sandboxes, helping them revitalize their organizations. And they provide consulting services to people who want to develop new systems.

All of the institute's offerings are directed toward building on the strengths of the five realities. In addition to using The Ringed Pentacle as a beacon, the partners draw upon a set of guidelines which they call "Rods of Power." These rods function both as walking sticks that provide assistance on this path of change, and as wands that enable the bearers to transform their lives. What follows are these guidelines.

Rods of Power
1. Regain Your Spirit.
2. Write Your Story.
3. Learn to Shapeshift.
4. Revitalize Your Sandbox.
5. Create a Wholesome System.

1. REGAIN YOUR SPIRIT

Sunny and her partners advocate shapeshifting as an avenue to organizational change. This approach poses a danger, however, because it involves giving your energy to a system by thoroughly identifying with it. If you go too far, you may identify so completely that you become totally absorbed by the system you want to change. When this happens, you lose your leverage and become ineffective. To reduce the chance of being co-opted, you need to get in touch with your spirit and find the center of your being.

Connecting with your spirit is also important because the purpose of changing organizations is to make them more supportive of you. To ensure proper support, it's essential that you get clear about who you are, what you want to accomplish, and what kind of support you need.

If you are unaccustomed to doing inner work you may find it difficult, at first, to get in touch with vital parts of yourself. The following questions are designed to provide assistance in locating the unique self that exists inside of you. Set aside some time to think about these questions.

Questions To Help You Regain Your Spirit

- What kind of a person are you?
- In what ways are you unique?
- What accomplishments give you a sense of pride?
- What beliefs do you cherish?
- What kinds of things do you value?
- What types of people do you enjoy?
- What's fun and exciting for you?
- What emotions do you express freely?
- What feelings do you hold back and why?
- When are you the most content?
- What were your favorite childhood pastimes?
- What place do you call home?
- Whom do you regard as heroes or heroines?

Imagine you are setting a place at the table for your higher self. Establish rituals to listen to your inner voice. Learn how to use your dreams and imagination to develop insight regarding your true nature.

2. WRITE YOUR STORY

Writing your story as you would like it to read signifies taking a giant step toward reclaiming your personal power. When you move from being a character in someone else's tale to becoming the author of your story you can say, "I am making conscious choices about the life I want to live. I am exercising influence over my life instead of performing a bit part as an object, a victim, or a passive bystander."

There is another reason why writing your story is important. To change systems, you have to be committed. To be committed, you have to know what you care about enough to sacrifice for. When you get clear about what really matters to you, a passion will be ignited to furnish the drive that's required for a long-term commitment.

The following questions will help you get started. Think about them, then record your thoughts.

Questions For Writing Your Life Story

- What is the major focus of your life?
  o What matters the most to you?
  o What roles do you play?
  o What would you select as a theme song for your life thus far?

Ask yourself, "What is my life all about?" If your life lacks a central theme, consider what you think about more than anything else and how you spend most of your time.

- What causes you pain or dissatisfaction?
  o What situations do you find stressful?
  o What things make you upset or angry?
  o What types of people annoy you?
  o What's missing in your life?
  o How frequently do you play roles that don't match who you are as a person?
  o To what degree are you living a story that doesn't fit?

Perhaps you are suffering from the shrink-to-fit syndrome by trying to adjust to situations that are too confining. Examine the borders in your present life. Ask yourself, "Where might I expand the borders so I have more room for me?" Take baby steps. Cross barriers you have perceived as impenetrable. Climb some hills you thought were insurmountable.

- What percentage of the time do you assertively take action as opposed to passively reacting to what happens?
  o To what extent do you take more than you give?
  o How often do you resist change in order to hold on to what you have?
  o Do you fulfill your need to belong by joining groups, knowing what you really need to do is commit to something you know is worthy of your support?
  o To what extent have you become lazy about learning?
  o When did you stop singing, dancing, and believing in magic?
  o How frequently do you rely on electronic messages as a substitute for face-to-face contact?
  o To what degree do you take for granted the environment in which you live?

Develop an observing self. Become more aware. As the author of your life story, you need to be actively engaged in making choices and decisions. You can't simply wait to see what unfolds. Practice risking by taking action on issues of importance to you. Create ceremonies to empower yourself.

Write Your Ideal Story

- What is your definition of happiness?
- How do you want to live your life?
- How would you like to spend your time?
- What would you like to accomplish during your lifetime?
- What would you like people to say about you after you die?
- Does your life need form and structure?
- Do you want more action and achievement?
- Would you like to be better connected?
- Do you need richer relationships?
- Do you need more energy and increased vitality?
- What kinds of work touch your heart by bringing out the joy in you and in others?
- How could you help make the world a better place?
- How can you live so you feel vibrant and alive every day?

Refer to "Part Two: Tales of Five Realities." Identify the aspects of these stories that you find appealing. Look for examples of people who are living these realities. Practice looking at the world through their eyes.

Accept the premise that you can create different states of being by changing your story. Practice saying to yourself, "There's more than one way to live my life. The old way is too stifling. I'm ready for a change."

Live Your Ideal Story

- What's required to make your ideal story a reality?
- How can you live the life that was meant for you?
- How can you live according to your beliefs and values?
- What experiences will expose you to more of what you want in your life?

Accept your place in the circle. Actively choose your life. Engage in experiences designed to point yourself in the desired direction. Design a plan. Set priorities. Take part in activities that are congruent with where you want to be.

Keep on the lookout for creeping inertia. Catch yourself every time something begins to interfere with following your chosen path. This can take the form of procrastinating, forgetting, getting sick, getting depressed, being too busy, getting too tired, finding irresistible diversions, yielding to the values and opinions of others, or becoming enmeshed in self-criticism.

If these things happen, take notice. Sit down and direct your awareness to what's occurring in your field of consciousness. Breathe deeply. Become fully aware of messages from your body. Silence your inner judge. Ask yourself, "Why am I not doing what I want to do?" Then wait patiently for the answer. Ideas, images, and memories will come. Practice rituals of inquiry and be patient. Eventually, positive movements will occur to take you in the direction you desire.

3. LEARN TO SHAPESHIFT

It's important to recognize that (a) you have an internal makeup that furnishes you with the ability to assume a wide variety of shapes; and (b) it's possible to change your shape, at will. Due to lack of use, certain capacities have weakened and you have lost some of your natural flexibility. To become a shapeshifter, you will need to restore the shapes that have atrophied.

How can you tell which shapes are strong and which are weak? A tool that will assist you is "A Profile of Your Shapes" (Appendix A). Complete the scale and note the shapes that receive the lower marks. Then focus on expanding these capacities.

What can you do to expand your weak shapes? The process of becoming a shapeshifter is a lot like rehearsing for a play. It requires you to practice thinking certain thoughts and engaging in specific behaviors. In this case you have five shapes; some tend to be oversized while others have shrunk. Your task is to build up the frail shapes.

One way to learn how to shapeshift is through exercise. Refer to "A Shapeshifting Exercise" (Appendix D). Another way is to look for people who can serve as role models and emulate their actions. Refer to "A Contemporary Shapeshifter" for one such model (Appendix E).

Yet, another way to become a shapeshifter is to look for opportunities to become more flexible within the five types of organizational systems. Each type reinforces a particular shape. The scale, "A Profile of an Organization's Shapes," will enable you to identify the shape of your current organization (Appendix B).

If your current organization supports one of your well developed shapes, you'll need to look elsewhere for arenas in which you can build up the shapes that are weak. You can use Appendix B to locate these arenas, as well.

How do organizations serve as arenas for shape-building? Each type poses a unique challenge. On page 106 is a chart that summarizes the central challenges of the realities on which the five types of organizations are based.

How can you meet these challenges and thereby restore the shapes that have atrophied? Here are some suggestions.

Experienced Organizers are able to accomplish a great deal even though they lack formal authority. Meet the challenge of "King of the Mountain" organizational systems by strengthening the infrastructure, establishing ground rules, and building solid frameworks. Introduce rituals. Abide by regulations. Keep track of details. Design new forms. Categorize records. Monitor operations. Be financially accountable. Get information to key decision makers. Take responsibility for outcomes.

The Central Challenges of Five Realities	
Realities	**The Challenges Are To:**
"King of the Mountain"	Lead without being on top.
"Motocross"	Compete without doing others in.
"White Water Rafting"	(1) Learn as much as you can without getting in over your head.
	(2) Be computer savvy without sacrificing face-to-face communication.
"Magical Mystery Mime Troupe and Jazz Band"	Love both yourself and others.
"Dance with Gaia"	Respect life in all its forms.

"Motocross" realities offer opportunities to become better Strategists in an atmosphere that requires you to demonstrate personal power, endurance, speed, and technical know-how. Take part in games that are fun and promote team spirit. Acquire allies, respect your opponents, and learn from your competitors. Take into account both qualitative and quantitative elements.

Meet the challenge of "White Water Rafting" realities to learn as much as you can by asking questions, listening to others, collecting useful information, developing an ability to correctly interpret information, benefiting from your mistakes, and welcoming feedback. Use computers as tools and become an active networker. Expand your interpersonal communication skills by engaging in discussions and dialogue. Learn how to negotiate agreements and facilitate meetings. Gain access to numerous communication channels.

The challenge of "Magical Mystery Mime Troupe and Jazz Band" realities to love both yourself and others offers an opportunity to link two poles. One way to connect these poles is to turn the opposing positions into a circle. Circular relationships move people and things from fixed points into ongoing processes.

For example, an either/or perspective yields:

(Either) for myself ——————————— (Or) for others

When you depict these characteristics as a both-and circle, they look like this:

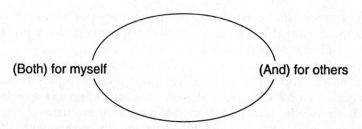

(Both) for myself   (And) for others

Honor different ways of looking at the world. Eliminate unnecessary conflicts by building structures based on harmony. Convene meetings to practice using tools for conflict management. Confront differences, not each other. Engage in exercises to reduce defensive behavior. Focus on common ground rather than on who is right and wrong.

Clarify your preferences about privacy and personal possessions at the same time you are committing to collaborative processes. Be aware that boundaries can be both functional and arbitrary. Invest in a vision that others share. Don't allow your ego to become attached to outcomes. Above all, maintain a sense of humor.

The challenge in "Dance with Gaia" realities is to respect life in all its forms. This challenge involves accepting the fact that you belong to a specific group, tribe, or nation, but you also belong to a worldwide community of human beings. Increase your understanding of and compassion for others. Devote time to some larger good. Look for ways to demonstrate your love for the planet. Make an effort to leave things better than they were when you found them.

By opening the door for numerous capacities to emerge and breathe, you become more whole as a person. After you strengthen your weak shapes, imagine there is an internal governing board convening inside of you where each shape has a vote. Then, carry on a discussion among this collection of capacities to consider which has the most to offer in a given situation.

4. REVITALIZE A SANDBOX

Once you have expanded your shapes, you are equipped to change an organization that you have identified as a sandbox. Change of this sort can be accomplished by completing the following steps.

STEP 1. Identify the grand reality of the sandbox you want to change.

Being part of an organization requires you to live out its particular story. Ask yourself, "What is the story of the reality on which this organization is based?" "To what extent does this sandbox represent a dysfunctional version of this story?" (Refer to "Part II: Tales of Five Realities.")

STEP 2. Understand how change is regarded within this organizational system.

It often happens that even change efforts that are positive, such as attempts to improve efficiency and effectiveness, are regarded with suspicion in sandboxes. Why is this the case?

One of the ways sandboxes maintain their existence is to resist change of any sort. They demand complete loyalty to preserving the status quo. Anyone who fails to demonstrate total allegiance may be regarded as a dissident and be subjected to ridicule or expulsion.

Sandboxes also resist change by preventing the people within them from communicating with each other about issues of importance. By employing a variety of divisive practices, sandboxes keep people separated from each other.

Taking into account the extent to which sandboxes reward stability and isolate people, changing them requires: (a) being perceived as a loyalist who is aligned with the current system; and (b) convincing the people in power that you want to connect with others for the purpose of strengthening the current system.

How can you build a case for change that will strengthen the current system? You need to identify a change target that fits the system's story and poses little threat to system's existence. You must also keep in mind what the preservers of that system will require in order to give your effort their blessing.

The following chart shows what is considered an appropriate focus of change and what is required to gain the support of a system's adherents. To change a sandbox, you need to align yourself with the targets and requirements listed below.

Key Considerations For Successful System Change		
Reality	**Focus of Change**	**Change Requirement**
"King of the Mountain"	Classification, Order	Must be methodical
"Motocross"	Action, Achievement	Must impact bottom line
"White Water Rafting"	Communication, Connection	Must improve a process
"Magical Mystery Mime Troupe and Jazz Band"	Relationship, Synergy	Must benefit both individuals and group
"Dance with Gaia"	Vitality, Ecology	Must be life-serving

STEP 3. Form a network composed of others who are part of this organization and who share your vision and dedication.

Why is it important to build a network? Lao Tzu says in the *Tao Te Ching*, "What's small is easy to scatter." System change requires a great deal of power and courage. When you connect with others your power increases substantially.

Your network should be composed of a cluster of three to seven people. Give yourself some time to think about the attributes you would like these people to possess. Then, look for compatriots wherever you go. If you overhear a conversation that indicates a potential link, say, "Excuse me, I couldn't help hearing what you were saying. I'm very interested in that, too."

Be patient. Everything about this process is evolutionary. It can't be forced. It's definitely not a quick fix. Links grow naturally until a critical mass forms.

STEP 4. Match the organizational system's energy.

Every system requires human energy to keep going. This energy is composed of three elements: a set of primary beliefs, a core commitment, and a basic purpose. To match a system's energy, assume its primary beliefs are true; embrace its core commitment; and support its basic purpose. The following chart shows how to match the energy in each of the five realities.

Matching a System's Energy			
Reality	**Primary Beliefs**	**Core Commitment**	**Basic Purpose**
"King of the Mountain"	Life is composed of structures and forms. The best is conventional.	Order	Control
"Motocross"	Life is a game. The best is out in front.	Results	Win
"White Water Rafting"	Life is communication. The best is balanced.	Learning	Exchange
"Magical Mystery Mime Troupe and Jazz Band"	Life is composed of many realities. The best is unbounded.	Community	Build lasting relationships
"Dance With Gaia"	Life is in everything. The best is natural.	The seventh generation	Restore and preserve the Earth's resources

You can also match the system's energy by collectively assuming the corresponding shape. The tool, "A Matrix of Individual and Organizational Shapes," will help you gauge the degree to which your shape corresponds to the shape of the organization of which you are a part (Appendix C).

STEP 5. Build on the system's strengths.

Work organizations possess the same potential strengths and weaknesses as the grand realities on which they are based. In healthy organizations the attributes outnumber the drawbacks. When their negative elements begin to outweigh their positive aspects, organizations become unhealthy. If this trend continues, the organizations turn into sandboxes.

Collectively examine the sandbox you want to change. Which reality, or combination of realities, does this sandbox represent? What are the strengths and weaknesses of this reality? In the company of your compatriots, find ways to build on the strengths until they outnumber the weaknesses.

What follows are some of the strengths and weaknesses of the five realities. The ideas will help you begin to identify attributes and drawbacks of the grand reality that represents the sandbox you want to change.

Strengths of "King of the Mountain"

"King of the Mountain" realities attest to the tradition of regarding rankings as natural. Structural hierarchies ensure role clarity and give people in leadership roles a sense of control.

Universal premises are accepted, out of which generalizations are made for specific situations. Processes are based on previous experiences. People assume that reason governs intelligent human actions.

Stability, consistency, and conformity give you a sense of safety and security. Naming and categorizing contribute to order. Form and formats are emphasized. Record-keeping and attention to detail promote accountability.

Rituals and routines provide continuity and strengthen personal identity. Regularly scheduled gatherings offer opportunities to get acquainted, find out how things are done, demonstrate loyalty, tap into valuable information sources, and know where you stand.

Sometimes it's wise to rest rather than risk. You need to lie low, be cautious, keep things simple, and maintain what you have. "King of the Mountain" realities offer opportunities to adopt a survival mode and depend on others.

Weaknesses of "King of the Mountain"

The primary drawback of "King of the Mountain" realities is their rigid structure. Hierarchies produce people who suffer from bureausis.

When this happens people lose their ability to think at a conceptual level and can't attend to anything greater than a sound bite.

Pyramids based on patriarchal contracts force people at the bottom to submit to those at the top. Top-down, high-control situations foster dependency and give rise to feelings of helplessness. Having access to special privileges cuts the leaders off from what's really going on by isolating them from the people below. In the presence of an excessive focus on the chain of command, people tend to look up for direction and shy away from taking personal responsibility.

Focusing on details interferes with strategic planning. A preoccupation with administrivia results in a great deal of red tape and wasted time. The very fact that a chain of command exists means it takes a long time to implement decisions.

Attempting to set up rules for everything is cumbersome and can backfire. In the absence of objectives and qualitative standards, everything comes down to ensuring there's enough to do, not whether the right things are getting done. People hold on to information as a way to preserve their power.

There's a tendency to resist change and cling to the past. Conformity fosters mediocrity. Risk aversion snuffs out creativity and leads to stagnation.

Strengths of "Motocross"

There are certain advantages to realities where everything is a race to the finish line. They offer opportunities to build ego strength, develop confrontation skills, become a better power broker, and learn from competitors.

The fast pace is stimulating. Rivalry creates tension and gives you an adrenalin rush. Winning makes you feel strong, powerful, and in control.

The pressure to come up with quick fixes forces you to increase your diagnostic skills. Making real-time decisions trains you to think quickly. You learn how to be more efficient, pragmatic, and results-oriented. Goal setting yields clear indicators of success. Achieving your objectives provides a sense of accomplishment.

"Motocross" realities are a lot like boot camp; they prepare you for combat. They show you how to deceive and outwit the enemy. They expose you to conditions that require you to develop courage and single-mindedness. They provide basic training in tactics, logistics, and survival. And they offer instruction in how to take the hill.

Technology plays a significant role in contemporary society. Therefore, it is very important to know how to use machines as tools while respecting human beings.

Weaknesses of "Motocross"

"Motocross" realities foster a mechanistic mindset; machines are regarded as more important than people. When people are treated as spare parts, their spirits are dampened and their motivation is crushed. It's assumed that every problem has a technological solution. If you're not an expert in something mechanical, you may feel like you're invisible.

A great deal of emphasis is placed on control through measurement. Everything has to be translated into numbers. Quantitative factors are more highly valued than are qualitative elements. Because values, feelings, and spiritual elements don't translate into numbers, they aren't regarded as important.

Sleep is perceived as a luxury because it is an unproductive use of time. Intense competition, combined with a desire to conquer the world, results in a race to coax as much as possible from one's body. People pride themselves on staying up all night to stay ahead of the curve. The danger is you may crash and burn.

The focus on personal achievement results in a proliferation of power-oriented egos. Competition rules out opportunities to collaborate. People are rewarded for being tough to the point of ruthlessness. Resources go to the most powerful rather than to the most promising.

"Motocross" realities foster specialization and compartmentalization. They deprive parts of their natural relationship to other parts. A strictly linear perspective rules out considering the possibility of multiple causes of problems. A utilitarian point of view means things have no value unless they can be immediately applied. Dualism serves as a breeding ground for divisiveness.

People assume there are no limits to how they can intervene in the natural world; they believe they can go anywhere and rearrange anything. This includes having the authority to alter the structure of human life, animal life, and the form of life itself.

Strengths of "White Water Rafting"

In "White Water Rafting" realities it seems as if the foundation is in constant motion. In the midst of a high degree of turbulence, people are drawn together to face a common opponent: rapid change.

The basic unit is small groups rather than individuals. The action-packed, rip-roaring environment forces you to pull together and become part of a highly responsive team.

You have complex roles that embrace many functions. This encourages you to share information. It also enlarges the number of things you can do and enables you to switch off responsibilities with others as the need arises. Tasks are interwoven and changeable, depending on the requirements placed on your group.

Solving problems involves examining interrelationships instead of looking for a single cause. Errors are minimized because the group at the place where an error occurs has the authority to take corrective action.

Satisfaction tends to be high due to the prevalence of self-management. Leadership is exercised more through facilitation than by decree. Cross-training supports skill diversification and yields flexibility.

To be successful, you engage in a vigorous learning process. Groups are regarded as learning centers. A primary goal is to develop groups of people who are capable of redesigning their processes to accommodate changing circumstances.

A major strength of these realities is their focus on communication. Regularly scheduled deliberations enable people to determine whether intergroup relations are promoting or impairing the group's effectiveness. Exchanging information supports innovation and creativity. Feedback provides a continual flow of information and ensures continuous improvement. Online networks open up boundaries and make it possible for you to connect. This ease of connection facilitates cross-cultural awareness and diversity. You can find out a lot about what's going on around the world.

Weaknesses of "White Water Rafting"

"White Water Rafting" realities encourage you to direct your attention to the information you obtain from computers. However, this is but a small fraction of the information that's available. Research studies show that a minority of leaders use computer-based information to make decisions. Most of them rely on face-to-face interaction, telephone conversations, and written documents. A critical question that is seldom answered is, "How do people acquire, interpret, share, and apply information?"

Experts are rewarded for possessing know-how regarding hardware and software technology, but not for demonstrating an understanding of human beings. In designing computer systems and databases they tend to ignore human needs. To be effective, computer systems should serve their users. The risk of building information systems that fail to include the human element is that people may not use them.

As a result of the way they have been trained, information technologists forget that gaining access to important data and using it wisely are more important to most people than is the latest computer application. For example, when installing new information systems or groupware, systems administrators frequently neglect to train the end users. When the users ask for help, the technologists treat them as irritants. Meanwhile, the users experience their own computer illiteracy and techno-incompetence as humbling and debilitating. Pleading for help makes them feel ashamed, defeated, and dumb.

Advances in information technology are of limited value where people equate sharing information with giving up their power. People must become information-oriented rather than power-oriented if information systems are to be fully utilized.

The web is a place where cleverness rules. Many users find depth and complexity boring. In the digital realm, messages may be composed of racial doctrines, diatribes, or personal attacks. Network newbies are harassed. Users flame everyone who disagrees with them.

Guaranteed anonymity fuels online monologues on the part of those for whom the prospect of actual meetings is too real. Many of these people use networks just to make their own voices heard by complete strangers. No one is accountable or responsible for what's being communicated. The web provides a means of individual expression that is not appropriate or acceptable in real life.

Unlimited information sharing may not work; it may result in data overload. It's important to distinguish between information and noninformation such as junk mail and rumors.

Computers isolate people from each other and contribute to alienation. Online correspondence that generates a morass of data is not the same as genuine communication. E-mail messages are no substitute for personal conversations. Being connected does not ensure a sense of belonging. Virtual communities can't take the place of authentic neighborhoods.

Strengths of "Magical Mystery Mime Troupe and Jazz Band"

Jazz musicians are self-organizing systems. While trying to complement each other, they collaborate and form alliances. The skills that are required to have a great jam session are exactly the kind of skills that leaders in this reality use to keep up with rapid change.

Closeness derives from respect, not obligation. Members devote time and energy to understanding and nurturing each other. Individual beliefs and values are shared by the group. As a member you have a sense of belonging to a community. Commitment and solidarity furnish antidotes to widespread feelings of separation and loneliness. United, you can achieve things that can't be accomplished alone.

The both-and principle helps you move away from rigid either/or formulas to more encompassing approaches. There is both an individual and a group focus. "What's in it for me?" is balanced with "What's in it for all of us?" Diversity is regarded as a resource. There's an assumption of abundance.

Boundaries are flexible. Spontaneity, fun, and magic are welcomed. Aesthetics is important. Vision and intuition are valued. Democratic principles are embraced. A focus on becoming a whole person promotes integration of your mind, body, and spirit.

Weaknesses of "Magical Mystery Mime Troupe and Jazz Band"

Building a community is very hard work. Being committed requires sticking it out through thick and thin. Because the path isn't linear, pursuing a dream isn't as easy as moving toward an objective.

In their eagerness to unite, people may adopt tribalistic practices, such as forming cults or developing closed languages. Individuals may hide behind the cover of the group. There's a danger of groupthink and a crowd mentality. Too much sameness can lead to mediocrity.

The lack of firm boundaries requires members to have excellent interpersonal skills. Tension can build up from trying to balance achieving group consensus with retaining your sense of self. Success calls for everyone to exhibit a high level of personal integrity.

Strengths of "Dance with Gaia"

"Dance with Gaia" realities support an Earth-based spirituality in which all forms of life are regarded as sacred. This belief permits you to tap into the Universal Power that's present in nature.

You learn to adopt a broad perspective and a long-term focus. A primary consideration is how what you do today can affect people in the future.

Realities of this type provide avenues for understanding and dealing with chaos. Change is the only constant. Extremely flexible structures come into being and people develop amazing resilience.

Ongoing partnerships are central, including a partnership with the environment. Ecoconsciousness is promoted. You develop a deep appreciation for the Earth's beauty.

By participating in a "Dance with Gaia" reality you become linked to a grand scheme because it fosters worldwide alliances and draws upon multi-cultural customs. There is a search for life-serving solutions to global problems.

Weaknesses of "Dance with Gaia"

The "Dance with Gaia" reality is complex. It doesn't fit the popular "KISS" admonition or the effort to reduce everything to its parts.

This reality is based on the concept of a universal family composed of all living things; however, nationalism is firmly entrenched. Most people think and behave locally. When they do make an effort to look at issues from a global perspective, they often become overwhelmed.

Success depends on alliances and alliances can be very fragile. They require you to relinquish a desire to dominate and subdue.

The risks are high because there are few precedents. To avoid getting stuck in a box, you have to be careful not to become cause-driven. Because there are no quick fixes in this reality, the results may be limited in terms of your lifetime.

STEP 6. Introduce strengths from other realities.

After revitalizing your sandbox by building on its strengths and helping it overcome its weaknesses, you are in a position to introduce strengths from other realities. In so doing, you will begin to make the system more wholesome.

How do you go about introducing strengths from other realities? Shamans who want to bring about healing and harmony develop such resonance with an entity that when they change their own behavior, the behavior of the entity changes as well. They accomplish this feat by merging with the entity's energy, knowing the entity from the inside, and changing it by directed intent. As a modern shapeshifter you follow in the footsteps of these shamans.

Let's say the sandbox you revitalized represents a "King of the Mountain" reality and you want to introduce some of the strengths of "White Water Rafting." To gain access to the strengths of the "White Water Rafting" reality, match its energy. Operate on the basis that life is communication and that the best is balanced. Embrace the core commitment and learn as much as you can. Support the exchange of information. (Refer to the chart, "Matching a System's Energy.")

A second way to gain access to the strengths of the "White Water Rafting" reality is to assume the shape of Communicators. Together, make a conscious effort to become educators, guides, facilitators, and navigators. (Refer to the chart, "The Ringed Pentacle" to determine the shape that corresponds to the reality you want to introduce. Refer to the sections, "Sunny Learns to Shapeshift" and "Circles of Influence" for descriptions of the five shapes.)

Expect change to be gradual because the current story has been developed by many people over a long period of time. Be patient. Keep a clear vision. Take pride in your work and enjoy what you are doing. Regard difficulties as normal and don't personalize them. Stay optimistic but expect progress to be difficult and slow. Concentrate on service and collective self-expression.

5. CREATE A WHOLESOME SYSTEM

Once you acquire the ability to assume all five shapes, understand the strengths of the five realities, and know how to revitalize a sandbox, you have the potential to create a wholesome system. This involves six steps.

STEP 1. Form partnerships.

How do you locate partners? After you get a concept of what you want, make a conscious decision to get the word out. Initiate conversations with everyone you meet . . . cab drivers, grocery clerks, gas station attendants, people waiting in lines, fellow art lovers, concert attendees, etc. Regard everyone as someone to talk to.

Advertise in publications that you read on a regular basis. Be a guest speaker on radio talk shows. Post notices on bulletin boards and kiosks near libraries and shops that you frequent.

STEP 2. Write your collective story.

Gather together your partners. Pool your ideas. Share and compare knowledge and experience. Write your group's ideal story.

Read the five stories. (Refer to "Part Two: Tales of Five Realities.") Analyze and discuss them. Observe how the plots are predetermined and how only certain roles are available. Examine the characters, settings, themes, symbols, and unifying threads.

Read and discuss the analytic summaries that follow. Use them as tools to write your story as you would like it to read.

"KING OF THE MOUNTAIN"—AN ANALYSIS

This is a story about a king who is an Organizer. He brings order by making rules and issuing proclamations. The plot depicts a young man who assumes responsibility for killing an evil giant in order to save his village. After he slays the giant he agrees to marry the princess on the condition they become friends, first.

A subplot is "Someday my prince will come." The king hopes to find a prince of a man who will become his son-in-law and the future leader of the kingdom.

The major theme of this story is "Life is composed of structures and forms." The king believes everything is under control as long as the villagers conform to the laws of the land. He adds structure by creating laws which he can enforce at his own discretion. The court administrators direct the affairs of state and control access to resources by establishing policies and procedures.

Various kinds of barriers are evident. The kingdom is surrounded on all sides by a wall. Intended to protect the villagers, it also serves as a barrier to external influence and change. A moat encircles the castle and geographically divides the haves from the have-nots. Ministers and gatekeepers separate the king from his subjects.

Another theme is "The best is conventional." Laws were established many years before King Rem's reign. The villagers assume that certain precedents will continue to exist, such as the notion that rank has its privileges. Knights who live in the castle have more power than farmers at the foot of the mountain.

By helping Eric locate the giant, the troll symbolizes how to lead without being on top. The troll has no formal authority but he has a great deal of power. He responds to Eric's needs in a very timely manner by providing information, assistance, and support. Erik's heroic deed would not have been possible had it not been for the troll's guidance.

Eric also leads without being on top. Instead of following the king's edict to marry the princess as a reward for his bravery, Eric agrees to the marriage on his own terms.

The gold key and the hawk represent good fortune (being in the right place at the right time). The sleeping giant symbolizes a very complex issue that can erupt into a major problem. The lottery gives the villagers hope that things will change for the better and illustrates the extent to which luck governs the fate of the people.

Unifying threads include:

Administrivia: Four layers of ministers manage the affairs of the court. Many serve as flak-catchers to shield the king.

Denial: The king did not tell anyone he was worried about the giant. As long as he didn't talk about it, he didn't have to face the potential problem. He could refuse to admit the level of his own anxiety.

The Good Life: King Rem and his family have everything they want. In spite of the fact that many of the villagers have to work two jobs to make ends meet, the king believes his subjects are satisfied.

Hierarchy: The entire village is organized by rank and class. Certain people are meant to lead; others are destined to follow. People are classified as superiors and subordinates within a centralized pyramidal structure. Even the king is threatened by a superior—the giant.

The In-Group: People who are well-connected enjoy special privileges. Although the villagers aren't supposed to leave the kingdom without the king's permission, Erik does so in order to destroy the giant. Because his brothers occupy positions of power, it never occurs to him he might be punished for disobeying one of the king's laws.

Nepotism: The king appoints his brothers to the top three positions in the kingdom. The villagers accept his practice of showing favoritism to relatives.

One Right Way: The king's way is the only way to do things. Punishment for disobedience includes banishment and marking.

Order: Soldiers and court administrators maintain the status quo. The villagers resist change and avoid risk. They feel safe doing everything the way it has always been done. The king thinks artists and musicians could threaten the existing order, so he channels their creativity into court-sponsored events.

Paternalism: The king regards his subjects as children. In exchange for his protection they are loyal and obedient. Although Eric couldn't save his father, he *could* save the king.

"Read My Mind" Leadership: By satisfying the king's unstated expectations, people prove their loyalty to him. The king was convinced the young man was trustworthy and noble because he appeared to read the king's mind.

"MOTOCROSS"—AN ANALYSIS

This story concerns a cross-country motorcycle contest open only to those who have qualified by accumulating a sufficient number of wins in previous races. All of the entrants are extremely experienced bikers, so the competition is fierce. Randy rides to win, no matter what the cost. Chris rides to develop his skill and to have fun. The plot pits the two friends against each other. After a race in which Randy behaves in an unsportsmanship manner, Chris drops him as a friend and gives up racing. Years later, Chris has a daughter who wants to participate in Motocross events. Chris is able to draw on his racing experience as he teaches his daughter.

One theme is "Life is a game." In the eyes of Randy, everything in life is a matter of winning or losing.

Another theme is "The best is out in front." Winners are those who will stop at nothing in an effort to finish first.

There are several symbols of achievement and action. Motocross serves as a symbol of war and dog-eat-dog competition. The motorcycles embody masculine power and control. Racing symbolizes freedom, speed, and personal drive. The steps Randy takes to improve his performance illustrate his skills as a Strategist. Chris represents a person who uses machines to have fun while respecting the people who operate them. Going dancing is a symbolic reward to Patty from Randy for being in his corner when he needs her.

Unifying threads include:

Dualism: There are a number of references to polarities such as up or down, winning or losing, strength or weakness, right or wrong, good or bad. Randy thinks people who are different from him are stupid or weird. He is quick to label anyone who fails to take a stand as "wishy-washy."

Friendship as Activity-Dependent: The two male characters are allies only when they're off the track. During a race all of the entrants are opponents.

Gaining the Competitive Edge: Randy keeps elaborate charts to ensure he is making progress. He focuses on meeting milestones in order to reach a more advanced stage. He knows it's important to do everything in his power to stay ahead of the pack.

One-Upmanship: One of the major attractions of this sport is that it offers opportunities to demonstrate personal power by outmaneuvering other bikers, causing them to spin their wheels, and forcing them out of the race. To win, the riders must gain advantage over their opponents.

Present Focus: That day's race is the only thing that matters to Randy. He doesn't give much thought to the potential effects of his actions.

Results-Driven: Winning is all that matters. The end justifies the means. Might makes right.

Risk Addiction: The riders express the excitement and thrill of riding in terms of being hooked on the exhilaration they feel when they go fast. Randy's motto is "Live hard and die young." He prides himself on living in the fast lane. He advises Chris to let up on the brakes and take more risks. The ultimate risk is to tempt Providence. The fact that the bikers are willing to risk death enhances the thrill of riding.

Ruthless Individualism: During the race it's every man for himself. The entrants are driven by a desire to contend with each other, even if this means getting hurt or injuring someone else.

Seizing the Spotlight: Victory means gaining everyone's attention in the winner's circle. It provides a few moments of fame and glory.

Survival of the Fittest: Only the toughest and best equipped bikers prevail.

Toughing It Out; No Pain, No Gain: Randy doesn't think he is working hard enough unless he is suffering physical discomfort. The competitors assume getting hurt is to be expected in any serious effort to improve their performance.

Winning through Intimidation: Randy knows the importance of exploiting every opportunity to make his power visible. He does this by psyching out his opponents even before the race begins.

Zero Sum: One party wins at the expense of another. Any gain made by one person diminishes the position of the other.

"WHITE WATER RAFTING"—AN ANALYSIS

This story concerns two people who go river rafting. The male character is an experienced rafter. The female character likes spontaneity and adventure. They meet through an electronic soccer network. There are eight guests. Two guides serve as navigators, trainers, facilitators, and reconnaissance experts.

The setting is a raging river in Idaho. The plot involves a ride through white water. All of the rafters learn to maintain control of their boats in the midst of turbulence. To do this requires them to listen carefully, correctly interpret information, and work as a team. When she falls out of the boat the other rafters act like this didn't happen. No one deals with it, directly.

One theme of the rafting story is "Life is communication." The two main characters communicate first by electronic mail then face-to-face. Their communication is rooted in similar interests such as soccer, adventure, and the outdoors. The rafters acquire skills to navigate the river by listening to the guides and by discussing each day's experiences around the campfire.

Another theme is balance. The female character works long hours and seldom takes vacation time. She goes on the rafting trip to bring some balance into her life. Successful navigation of the river depends on the rafters' ability to keep the boats balanced. The guides balance the work of paddling with time off to eat and relax.

The river is a symbol for life. Crashing through powerful holes, climbing large waves, tackling tumultuous rapids, and navigating steep narrow chutes all symbolize risk-taking and innovation. Making an excursion into a world few realize exists represents going into one's self.

The fact that the two main characters have no names is symbolic of the way the human element is neglected in information-oriented groups. People are often left out of the loop in high tech settings.

Unifying threads include:

Communication: The primary unifying thread in this story is communication. He and she meet by communicating electronically. When it comes to things that really matter, however, their interpersonal communication breaks down.

> The guides confer before taking on the waterfalls, then share their decision with the other rafters. They methodically explain what to expect and answer questions the rafters pose. All of the members of the group sit around the campfire and talk each night. The river speaks to them, warning of what lies ahead.

Feedback: She learns to paddle a boat and swim, based on feedback she gets from him. Her body lets her know she is exercising seldom-used muscles. The rafters depend on immediate feedback from the river as they maneuver their boats through the white water. The trip gives the rafters a chance to say things to each other that they might not say otherwise.

Give-and-Take: He exchanges his skill as an experienced rafter for the cost of two passages. The guides exchange their skills for payment from the guests.

Learning: All of the guests acquire rafting skills. They improve their ability to listen to the river and to each other. They discover what it means to take physical risks. And they begin to look at their careers and their lives with new eyes.

> She learns that E-mail gave her a false sense of trust. Online messages led her to believe she would be able to converse with him in person. She learns that she needs to ask more questions and take less for granted. And she learns not to mistake the thrill of adventure for foolhardiness.

"MAGICAL MYSTERY MIME TROUPE AND JAZZ BAND"—AN ANALYSIS

This is a tale about seclusion and attachment. The plot involves a person who is struggling to retain a sense of individuality while developing a feeling of commitment to a small group of friends.

The story takes place in both an urban area and in the country. The central characters include the narrator and a group of friends, all of whom work in the city. Gatherings are held at a ranch located on ten acres of rolling hills.

One theme is "Life is composed of many realities." Both everyday occurrences and dreams are important to the narrator. Sabrina serves as a Bridge between different realities. She shows the narrator how to be in touch with both the rational and the occult. She links the dream state with being awake. Another theme is "The best is unbounded." The narrator, who is accustomed to having a lot of private space, begins to let down some personal barriers during the process of building stronger ties to other people. The narrator also becomes a Bridge between people in prison and the outside world.

The symbols are explained in the text. They include a journey as a symbol for life. The cart is a symbol for getting away and moving on. The horse refers to unconscious energy. The moon is a call to enter the darkness and make a journey into the labyrinth. The game signifies the game of life. Rules encourage making changes in the way one is structuring life. Card games suggest playing the game of life with one's current hand. The shaman symbolizes healing.

Unifying threads include:

A Both-And Perspective: As the narrator moves from an egocentric existence to a more collaborative lifestyle, this individual adopts a schedule that includes both time alone and gatherings with other people. This change requires being both a friend to self as well as a friend to others. The sex of the narrator is not identified so that this person can be imagined by the reader as both male and female.

Boundaries: The boundary between dreams and reality becomes fuzzy. Difficulties that arise when interpersonal boundaries become unclear are alluded to in two situations: Sabrina borrows a costume and fails to return it. Peter evidences tribalistic tendencies when he expresses his opposition to inviting strangers to the gatherings.

Community: Through frequent interactions and explorations of shared interests, the group members discover common ground. Bonding gives them a sense of unity.

The Journey is its Own Reward: The intent of the mime troupe and jazz band is to travel and have fun. The travelers engage in a wide variety of performances, intending to make everyone a star.

Paradox: The narrator finds increased strength by becoming more vulnerable. And by relinquishing an attachment to personal possessions, this character gains an increased sense of security.

Wholeness: Together, the characters illustrate that "The whole is greater than the sum of its parts." As a group, they achieve results far beyond what they can accomplish as individuals. Due to associations with people in two small communities, the narrator develops into a more complete person.

"DANCE WITH GAIA"—AN ANALYSIS

The setting in this story is a presentation by an astronaut who has seen the Earth from the surface of the moon. As an ecological evangelist, she travels all over the world, giving speeches and showing films taken from space.

One theme of the story is "Life is in everything." Marin tries to help others see that all things in nature are alive, that all life is sacred, and that all living things have a place in the great circle of life.

Another theme is "The best is natural." Marin encourages people to find ways to live so they are close to the land. Gaia is a symbol for the Earth. Marin represents what it means to be A Friend of Gaia. Her purpose is to make the world a better place by helping to build a sustainable society. She believes it's important for people to meet their own needs without jeopardizing the needs of those who will be alive seven generations from now.

The astronauts' accounts of their trips into outer space serve as testimonials to the fact we are all part of something larger than ourselves. The Earth's gravitational pull symbolizes the natural attraction all things have toward each other. Not being able to see any boundaries on the Earth from space points to our need to transcend egos and tribalism so we can work for the good of the planet as a whole. The example of the ants makes the point that small perturbations can be amplified into very significant changes. Lightning is symbolic of the energy that exists in nature and of how quickly things can spread around the planet.

Unifying threads include:

Co-Evolution: The astronauts share many experiences during their trips into space and these shared moments cause them to gain a much broader perspective of what is happening back home on planet Earth. They change in ways that are mutually advantageous.

The title of this story infers a partnership between human beings and the Earth in which both reach a highly developed state through growth and change. This process is referred to as a dance because, ideally, it is rhythmic and harmonious.

Ecosystem: Marin refers to the interrelationship among all of the elements that make up the Earth. She points out how human activities have damaged the atmosphere, a fragile ribbon that surrounds our planet.

Gaia Consciousness: Knowledge of what is happening to the Earth as a whole is very important to the central character. She has dedicated herself to telling others what she has seen taking place on the planet from the vantage point of the moon.

The Gaia Hypothesis: This formulation postulates that everything on the Earth's surface is part of a self-regulating system. The environment co-evolves with the biological life forms that inhabit the planet.

Global Citizenship: Based on her experiences as an astronaut, the central character believes the entire planet is at risk. She hopes to increase the amount of responsibility people are willing to take for restoring the Earth's health and beauty.

Vitality: Marin is full of life and vigor. As an evangelist she renews and refreshes those who attend her presentations. The story suggests human beings can tap the energy in nature to accomplish extraordinary things.

STEP 3. Incorporate strengths from all five stories.

The best insurance against an organization becoming unhealthy is to include positive aspects of all five systems. This will make it wholesome. Refer to "A Wholesome Organization" (Appendix F). It describes an enterprise that represents the best of five systems.

STEP 4. Assume the shapes that will support your collective story.

Acting in concert, call forth all five realities by giving them energy. Collectively assume the shapes that will bring your story to life.

STEP 5. Prevent the growth and development of a sandbox.

Monitor the process. Revisit your creation regularly. Conduct periodic check-ups to keep your system healthy and responsive. Build in checkpoints and rituals to collaboratively re-evaluate ways to draw upon the strengths of all five systems and minimize the weaknesses.

STEP 6. Play on the edge.

Learn to play on the edge of the unformed. Look at life as a multi-faceted process rather than as a dot-to-dot, one-dimensional procedure of meeting goals and satisfying desires. Regard what you are doing as a project-in-progress. Co-evolve with your partners and with your project.

As you play on the edge you will not always be able to control what happens. Part of the evolutionary process is to be flexible when the unexpected occurs. Choose to work at what you love then make use of what life happens to bring your way. Be open to mystery and the unexpected. Anticipate luck and make it work for you. Welcome the deep knowing and guidance that come from the universe. Continue to shift your shape to take advantage of the winds of fate.

There is a story that concerns two people who chose to work at what they loved, then made use of what life brought their way. After reading this example, watch for other situations where people are successfully playing on the edge of the unformed.

A SHORT TALE

On the Mendocino Coast north of Gualala, California, there is an inn and restaurant called St. Orres. Driving that stretch of Highway One, you can't miss its exotic Russian-style domes. The history of this inn is as enchanting as its physical allure, for it involves two people who charted their own course then took advantage of the winds of fate.

Intending to open a toy factory, Eric and Ted Black decided to build a captivating, storybook structure that would reflect their products. So, they designed a large wood and timber lodge to convey an atmosphere of fantasy and playfulness. While the facility was under construction their money ran out. To restore their cash flow they began serving food to the people who stopped by to take photographs of the unusual onion domes.

Two years after they had begun the original toy making venture, the owners hired a full-time chef and opened the building to overnight guests. Now, twenty-one years later, they have eight guest rooms in the main building and eleven cottages on fifty acres of redwoods.

The chef has been honored by the James Beard Foundation and the accommodations have been featured in countless articles about North Coast inns. A guest book at the reception desk is full of comments extolling St. Orres' virtues, such as "We discovered a romantic hideaway;" "The dining was exquisite;" "Without exception, the rooms have provided us with a home away from home;" and "This is a tremendously healing place."

APPENDIX A. A PROFILE OF YOUR SHAPES

This scale will help you assess your shapes. A high degree of flexibility is evident when your scores for all five shapes are in the 25-35 range. A score below 25 indicates a shape that needs to be strengthened. An over-developed shape is indicated by a score over 35. (Make copies of this scale and save the original for future use.)

INSTRUCTIONS: RANK ORDER ALL FIVE CHOICES UNDER EACH SELECTION. PUT A "5" IN FRONT OF THE CHOICE THAT BEST DESCRIBES YOU, A "4" IN FRONT OF THE CHOICE THAT NEXT BEST DESCRIBES YOU, ETC.

1. I prefer to operate by:

   a._____ Having a secure position and knowing where I stand.
   b._____ Playing a key role in the exchange of information.
   c._____ Participating in a community where people share responsibilities and the fruits of their labor.
   d._____ Being a member of a global partnership dedicated to healing the planet.
   e._____ Working in a group that runs efficiently and achieves its goals.

2. One of my strongest assets is:

   a._____ I enjoy both working alone and with others.
   b._____ I think of the long term implications of my actions.
   c._____ I am extremely detail oriented.
   d._____ I am an excellent communicator.
   e._____ I am a masterful troubleshooter.

3. I am highly motivated by:

   a._____ Opportunities to learn.
   b._____ The potential to advance.
   c._____ Belonging to a close-knit, committed group.
   d._____ Leaving things better than they were when I found them.
   e._____ A fast pace and the thrill of meeting challenges.

4. I gain the most satisfaction from:

   a._____ Bringing order to messy situations.
   b._____ Working collaboratively with others who share my values, beliefs, and interests.
   c._____ Making progress toward an objective.
   d._____ Exchanging information with others through E-mail.
   e._____ Gaining first hand experience of what's going on in different parts of the world.

5. I think it's very important to:

    a._____ Look out for the good of the whole.
    b._____ Demonstrate loyalty, caution, and restraint.
    c._____ Preserve the ecosystem.
    d._____ Be connected online.
    e._____ Align with people in power.

6. Above all, I would like to:

    a._____ Make a difference in the world.
    b._____ Light fires under people and do the impossible.
    c._____ Be someone others look up to; have prestige and position power.
    d._____ Learn as much as I can.
    e._____ Build long-term relationships.

7. I think it's essential for a good leader to:

    a._____ Promote continuous improvement.
    b._____ Possess technical know-how.
    c._____ Act with personal integrity.
    d._____ Demonstrate power and authority.
    e._____ Build consensus.

8. I prefer to work with people who:

    a._____ Make it a practice to give something back to the planet.
    b._____ Possess a can-do attitude.
    c._____ Are concerned about the welfare of others.
    d._____ Are well-informed.
    e._____ Are like me.

9. I have a reputation for:

    a._____ Leading productive meetings.
    b._____ Understanding the global impact of local decisions and actions.
    c._____ Winning battles.
    d._____ Getting information to those who need it to do their jobs.
    e._____ Facilitating agreements among people who see things differently.

10. I think one of the biggest mistakes you can make is:

    a._____ Not taking into consideration how decisions can negatively affect the environment.

    b._____ Not being a strong competitor.

    c._____ Not asking for feedback.

    d._____ Not following a tried and true approach.

    e._____ Not understanding the value of democratic principles.

11. I tackle problems by:

    a._____ Using them to bring people together.

    b._____ Looking for poor connections and places where information fell through the cracks.

    c._____ Regarding them as signals of a need to develop new systems.

    d._____ Implementing the best quick fix.

    e._____ Trying to find out who made a mistake.

12. I like to work in places where:

    a._____ There is a high level of competition and star performers are rewarded.

    b._____ Things are stable and there are few surprises.

    c._____ The focus is on life serving products and services.

    d._____ There is a sense of belonging.

    e._____ People are self-managed.

A PROFILE OF YOUR SHAPES

SCORE SHEET

SCORING INSTRUCTIONS: GO ACROSS, RECORDING THE NUMERICAL RANKING BESIDE EACH LETTER. FOR EXAMPLE, IN THE FIRST SELECTION IF YOU RANKED ITEM "A" AS SECOND, THEN RECORD "2" IN THE SPACE TO THE RIGHT OF "A" ON THE SCORE SHEET. IF YOU RANKED ITEM "E" AS FOURTH, RECORD "4" IN THE SPACE TO THE RIGHT OF "E."

AFTER RECORDING ALL OF YOUR RESPONSES, ADD EACH COLUMN. THE COLUMN WITH THE HIGHEST SCORE INDICATES YOUR STRONGEST SHAPE.

1.	a___	e___	b___	c___	d___
2.	c___	e___	d___	a___	b___
3.	b___	e___	a___	c___	d___
4.	a___	c___	d___	b___	e___
5.	b___	e___	d___	a___	c___
6.	c___	b___	d___	e___	a___
7.	d___	b___	a___	e___	c___
8.	e___	b___	d___	c___	a___
9.	a___	c___	d___	e___	b___
10.	d___	b___	c___	e___	a___
11.	e___	d___	b___	a___	c___
12.	b___	a___	e___	d___	c___
Totals:	___	___	___	___	___
	Organizer	Strategist	Communicator	Bridge	Friend of Gaia

APPENDIX B. A PROFILE OF AN ORGANIZATION'S SHAPES

This scale will help you evaluate the shapes of an organization. After evaluating your current work organization, use the scale to identify what would be an ideal work setting for you. Then compare the real with the ideal. (Make copies of this scale and save the original.)

INSTRUCTIONS: RANK ORDER YOUR RESPONSES TO EACH OF THE FOLLOWING ITEMS. RATE THE ITEM THAT IS MOST CHARACTERISTIC OF YOUR ORGANIZATION HIGHEST (5). RATE THE LEAST CHARACTERISTIC ITEM LOWEST (1).

1. The structure of this organization is:

a._____ A worldwide alliance that reflects many cultures.

b._____ A traditional hierarchy.

c._____ A network of integrated self-managed teams.

d._____ A series of ad hoc project teams.

e._____ A community of interdependent entrepreneurs.

2. The mission of this organization is to:

a._____ Stay on course by responding to feedback.

b._____ Build a strong community and explore innovative ways to exchange goods and services.

c._____ Be first at the least cost.

d._____ Develop sufficient social, economic, and political clout to deal with global issues.

e._____ Get everyone singing from the same hymnbook and maintain a steady business.

3. This organization's philosophy is based on the following themes:

a._____ Rank has its privileges.
Form should precede function.
Don't make waves.

b._____ The end justifies the means.
Business is war.
If it ain't broke, don't fix it.

c._____ The whole is greater than the sum of its parts.
Leadership involves improving the human condition.
Look for the big picture.

d._____ There is no failure, only feedback.
Communication controls our fate.
Keep your ear to the ground.

e._____ Small is beautiful.
Business is a powerful force that can be harnessed for economic and social change.
Restore the Earth's beauty by becoming a global citizen.

4. The environment this organization operates in is:

a._____ Changing slowly in some ways; rapidly in others. The changes are both predictable and unpredictable.
b._____ Changing rapidly in predictable ways.
c._____ Extremely chaotic; change is the only constant.
d._____ Highly stable; nothing much ever changes.
e._____ Changing slowly in very predictable ways.

5. The market for this organization's products and services can best be described as:

a._____ The demand for both superior products and quality service is both short and long term.
b._____ Short-term; the pressure to come out with new products for the next quarter is unrelenting.
c._____ Real-time; the demand for products and services must be met immediately.
d._____ Constant and steady; the demand for products doesn't vary much.
e._____ Long-term; the demand is for life-serving products and services.

6. Elements that are highly valued in this organization include:

a._____ Tradition, authority, compliance, continuity, order, and rituals.
b._____ Complexity, resilience, and vitality.
c._____ Results, efficiency, precision, action, force, and know-how.
d._____ Vision, ethics, intuition, cohesion, harmony, and trust.
e._____ Information, networks, self-management, exchange, and cross-training.

7. Control is exercised through:

a._____ Prediction, analysis, measurement, and error correction.
b._____ Understanding complexity and making use of the order that exists in chaos.
c._____ Establishing standard operating procedures and monitoring individual performance.
d._____ Shared responsibility and mutual trust.
e._____ Dissemination of information and feedback loops.

8. People in this organization plan by:

    a._____ Thinking globally and acting locally.

    b._____ Charting a course based on what's happening in the external environment.

    c._____ Reframing situations, creating alternative scenarios, and considering a wide range of options.

    d._____ Making forecasts based on linear trends and cumulative forces.

    e._____ Looking to the past for indications of what to do in the present.

9. Human beings are regarded as:

    a._____ Resources to be utilized.

    b._____ Unpredictable entities who need to be supervised.

    c._____ Partners in a global enterprise.

    d._____ Sources of knowledge and information.

    e._____ Members of a community.

10. Above all, leaders in this organization need to:

    a._____ Be actively involved in what's going on around the world.

    b._____ Be part of the establishment.

    c._____ Provide data, manage interfaces, and keep the channels of communication open.

    d._____ Take charge.

    e._____ Have a strong sense of purpose, build consensus, encourage commitment, and create a sense of community.

11. Power is associated with:

    a._____ Class, title, image, prestige, reputation, and possessing material goods.

    b._____ Intimidating, winning, and possessing know-how.

    c._____ Communicating, connecting, exchanging, and possessing information.

    d._____ Individual commitment and group solidarity.

    e._____ Global affiliations.

12. Change is viewed as:

    a._____ The only constant.

    b._____ Essential for personal and organizational renewal.

    c._____ Necessary for continuous improvement.

    d._____ Expansion or reduction.

    e._____ A threat to the status quo.

Appendix B

A PROFILE OF AN ORGANIZATION'S SHAPES

SCORE SHEET

SCORING INSTRUCTIONS: FOR EACH ITEM, GO ACROSS, RECORDING THE NUMERICAL RANKING BESIDE EACH LETTER. FOR EXAMPLE, IN THE FIRST SELECTION IF YOU RANKED ITEM "B" AS SECOND, THEN RECORD "2" IN THE SPACE NEXT TO "B." IF YOU RANKED ITEM "D" AS FOURTH, RECORD "4" IN THE SPACE NEXT TO "D."

AFTER RECORDING ALL OF YOUR RESPONSES, ADD EACH COLUMN.

1.	b____	d____	c____	e____	a____
2.	e____	c____	a____	b____	d____
3.	a____	b____	d____	c____	e____
4.	d____	e____	b____	a____	c____
5.	d____	b____	c____	a____	e____
6.	a____	c____	e____	d____	b____
7.	c____	a____	e____	d____	b____
8.	e____	d____	b____	c____	a____
9.	b____	a____	d____	e____	c____
10.	b____	d____	c____	e____	a____
11.	a____	b____	c____	d____	e____
12.	e____	d____	c____	b____	a____
Totals:	____	____	____	____	____
	Pyramid	Arrow	Web	Mosaic	Sphere
	(Contract-based)	(Market-driven)	(Information-oriented)	(Community-focused)	(Earth-centered)

APPENDIX C. A MATRIX OF INDIVIDUAL AND ORGANIZATIONAL SHAPES

This matrix will give you a snapshot of the similarity, or lack thereof, between your shapes and those of an organization. If the two profiles are nearly the same, there may be few opportunities in this organization for you to increase your flexibility. On the other hand, if similarity is completely lacking, you may be very frustrated because your capabilities are not valued.

INSTRUCTIONS: RECORD YOUR SCORES FROM THE "PROFILE OF YOUR SHAPES." PUT AN X IN EACH "I" COLUMN ACROSS FROM THE APPROPRIATE NUMBERS. DO THE SAME FOR THE SCALE, "A PROFILE OF YOUR ORGANIZATION'S SHAPES," PUTTING AN X IN EACH "O" COLUMN ACROSS FROM THE APPROPRIATE NUMBERS.

CONNECT THE "I" POINTS WITH A PEN OF ONE COLOR. CONNECT THE "O" POINTS WITH A PEN OF A DIFFERENT COLOR.

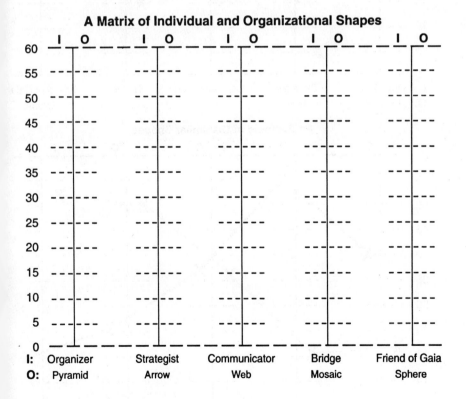

A Matrix of Individual and Organizational Shapes

	Organizer	Strategist	Communicator	Bridge	Friend of Gaia
I:	Organizer	Strategist	Communicator	Bridge	Friend of Gaia
O:	Pyramid	Arrow	Web	Mosaic	Sphere

Appendix C

A Matrix of Individual and Organizational Shapes

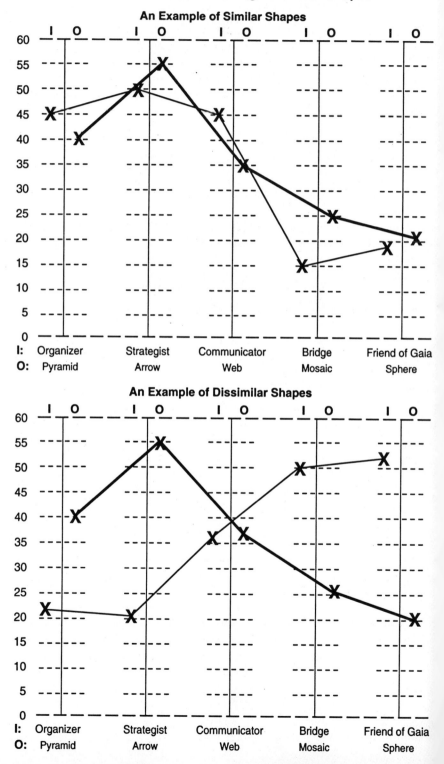

An Example of Similar Shapes

I: Organizer   Strategist   Communicator   Bridge   Friend of Gaia
O: Pyramid   Arrow   Web   Mosaic   Sphere

An Example of Dissimilar Shapes

I: Organizer   Strategist   Communicator   Bridge   Friend of Gaia
O: Pyramid   Arrow   Web   Mosaic   Sphere

APPENDIX D. A SHAPESHIFTING EXERCISE

You can read this book from a variety of perspectives. Five options present themselves.

First, you may use the book as a guide to identifying, naming, and categorizing organizational systems. When you read it for this purpose it defines, gives form, and lends order.

A second option is to read the book as a manual of personal change strategies. Remedies that are advocated include expanding your thought processes, enlarging your action patterns, and embracing internal diversity.

A third alternative is to use the book to spur an exchange of ideas with other people, or as a buffer to broach a topic that is difficult to talk about. Many of the ideas in this book are controversial; they are intended to stimulate discussion.

Use the book as a vehicle to engender exchange. Share it with your spouse, partner, children, relatives, friends, and clients. Discuss the concepts, ideas, and proposed remedies. Ask "Are the assertions credible?" "Do I agree with the ideas presented?" "What evidence is there to support or refute the positions taken?" "How useful are the strategies for changing the organizations of which I am a part?"

Initiate conversations with others about the concepts you find especially provocative. For example, do you believe rituals are important? Is stability, in itself, an indicator of success? Do computers pose a threat? Have you dealt with both-and dilemmas such as trying to be both separate and attached, both free and secure, or both realistic and idealistic? Do you believe some issues are so complex and comprehensive that they require us to regard the world as borderless?

Fourth, you can approach the material as a story. Test it against your own experience. Are you embroiled in office politics and infighting? Is your freedom cut off because you're trapped in a box? Is your creativity stifled? Do you feel unfulfilled, bored, or burned out? Are you weary of other's expectations defining your destiny? Has the thrill of the corporate chase faded? Did you expect to achieve more than you have at this point in your life? Has your marriage unraveled? Are you missing a sense of belonging? Do you sense a pressing need to clarify what is really important? Have you ever taken a road trip or fantasized about going on the road for an extended period of time? Do you dream about finding a new way to live and work?

A fifth way to read this book is from the standpoint of a caretaker of the Earth who wants to build a stronger link with the environment. The book points to the importance of learning how to live on the planet in such a way that you add value to, rather than diminish, the available resources. It shows how to increase your energy level by fully tapping into the planet's power sources, such as the beauty in nature and the life force that resides in everything around you.

Each of the five vantage points from which you can read this book calls forth a specific shape. When you use the book as a guide to give order you expand your capacity as an Organizer. During the process of pragmatically examining the contents from the standpoint of a personal change strategy you toughen your skills as a Strategist. By drawing upon the ideas as a way to stimulate discussion you intensify your internal Communicator. As a story, the book encourages you to tap your capacity to imagine new worlds, connect with fellow explorers, and serve as a Bridge between traditional approaches and innovative ways to live. Your capacity to assume the shape of a Friend of Gaia is nourished whenever you embrace ways to restore the Earth's resources and beauty.

For maximum benefit read the book more than once, consciously adopting a different perspective with each reading. For example, read the book as a directory of ways to categorize organizations and record what seems important to you. Then read it as a story and compare it to your own life. What distinctions can you make between the two readings? What differences can you identify in terms of what you took away? Refer to the chart, "Matching a System's Energy." To what extent were you aware of changes in the focus of your energy?

The ultimate payoff to reading this book from multiple vantage points is an increase in your internal flexibility. With each spin you change your outlook. As you outlook alters, so do your thoughts and impressions. Eventually, your appearance and actions may change as well.

With practice you can learn to consciously change the shape of your being. Knowing how to bring about change within yourself at this level is a tremendously powerful capability!

And that's not all. This power can be drawn upon to change the larger entities of which you are a part. Once you know how to change yourself you will be empowered to shape the systems around you. So, at a sixth level you can read this book to glean ideas about shifting your shape as a way to shape the world of the future.

APPENDIX E. A CONTEMPORARY SHAPESHIFTER

Then trading shapes again.

GARY SNYDER
"T-2 Tanker Blues"
Riprap and Cold Mountain Poems

Gary Snyder, a poet, is an individual who possesses the ability to assume all five shapes. The following points illustrate his flexibility.

ORGANIZER

• His values are based on a long-standing tradition:

"As a poet I hold the most archaic values on earth. They go back to the upper Paleolithic: the fertility of the soil, the magic of animals, the power-vision in solitude, the terrifying initiation and rebirth, the love and ecstasy of the dance, the common work of the tribe."[5]

• Through his poems and essays he makes sense of confusion by creating form and giving order. He imparts ideas, provides information, furnishes structure, and recommends solutions.
• By giving basic instructions for living he gives people grounding.
• Although he has little formal authority he exerts influence and accomplishes a great deal.
• He writes in the classic tradition using simple, direct statements. The account of his life's journey, *Mountains and Rivers Without End* (1996), is told as an epic poem.
• He maintains a stable life in the foothills of the Sierras in northern California.

STRATEGIST

• He enjoys fixing his 1958 Willys pickup truck.
• He has worked as a logger, lumberjack, fire lookout, and forestry inspector. As a trail crew laborer he used shovels, picks, and dynamite. He spent nine months in the engine room of a tanker in the Pacific Ocean and the Persian Gulf.
• He respects human beings while using machines as tools. His book of poems entitled, *Axe Handles,* points to how man alone uses tools to make tools.
• His poems attest to his devotion to work.
• He makes efficient use of tools and equipment through collective ownership and recycling.
• He advocates embracing science and technology.

• *Riprap and Cold Mountain Poems* is read by trail crews in work camps in the back country. They appreciate the poems "as much for their sweat as their art."

• He is an activist who urges others to become involved politically at the local level by getting a sense of workable territory and beginning to act, taking one step at a time.

COMMUNICATOR

• He possesses exemplary communication skills and employs a variety of avenues in his writing, including lyric poems, riddles, narratives, and essays.

• His work is grounded in an oral tradition that holds poems, stories, and myths as common treasures.

• As a teacher at the University of California at Davis he serves as a conduit for information.

• He is a lifelong learner. He graduated from Reed College with a degree in anthropology and literature. He was the recipient of a Bollingen Foundation research grant. In order to be knowledgeable about many things he "does his homework."

• He is connected online and communicates by electronic mail.

• He maintains that a poet "must have total sensitivity to the inner potentials of his own language . . . an ear, an eye, and a belly."

BRIDGE

• He serves as a bridge between the East and the West. From 1956 to 1968 he studied Zen Buddhism in Japanese monasteries. While he lives by the Buddhist precept to cause the least possible harm, his work is grounded in Poundian modernism and he has an intimate knowledge of the American West.

• As a bridge between reality and fantasy he was as the model for Japhy Ryder, the hero in Jack Kerouac's *The Dharma Bums.*

• By being able to write as both the Worker and the Thinker he creates a fertile whole.

• He negotiates boundaries, finds common ground, and functions as a cultural broker between political and social groups.

• He suggests that computer technicians could lead balanced lives if they ran technology part of the year and walked with elk the rest. The following passage further demonstrates his value of balance:

> "Learn to break the habit of unnecessary possessions . . . but avoid a self-abnegating anti-joyous self-righteousness. Simplicity is light, carefree, neat and loving—not a self-punishing ascetic trip."[6]

• He draws upon both conventional wisdom and intuition.

• He pursues both inner harmony and worldly success. He embraces the principle that "true affluence is not needing anything." Concurrently, he is a member of the American Academy of Arts and Letters. In 1974 he won the Pulitzer Prize for *Turtle Island*.

• *Axe Handles* points to the roots of community in the family and explores the transmission of cultural values and knowledge.

• He lives with his family and friends and advocates a communal life-style. He supports the exploration of alternative social structures, such as extended families, where there are fewer children and everyone shares child care. He says the creation of new selves, new relationships, and new world of beings is just as important as reproduction.

• He embraces Jeffersonian democracy and believes it's important to have a sense of place and to care about what goes on in your backyard.

• He is involved in the Yuba Watershed Institute, a community group that works to understand and protect the ecosystem.

• An image of oneness is a major theme throughout his work. He sees the whole universe as mutually reflecting and mutually embracing. Nature is composed of interconnected life forms, all of equal moral and spiritual standing.

• Based on the Native American myth of Kokopelli, the hump-backed flute player, he depicts the role of a poet as a wandering poet-minstrel with a backpack.

FRIEND OF GAIA

• He gains energy from nature. "The voice that speaks to me as a poet . . . is the voice of nature herself."[7]

• He urges us to observe nature carefully and to see ecology, bioregional-ism, and sustainable culture as intrinsically bound to our own human fate.

• He has a long-term perspective. It took forty years to write his epic poem, *Mountains and Rivers Without End*. During these years he said he was patient and never anxious because he trusted the poem to work itself out.

• As a poet he employs an organic method, allowing each poem to follow its grain and flow from an "energy-mind-field-dance."

• He claims that much of his work is to let a poem grow and speak for itself.

• Circles play a major role in his writing. A key metaphor is the exchange of energy in the circle of life and death.

• He believes that optimum population should be based on a sense of total ecological health, including the wildlife population.

• He thinks economics ought to be a sub-branch of ecology.

• Throughout his life he has promoted the position of man as the "gentle steward of the earth's community of being." He co-founded the program on nature and culture at U.C. Davis. He is active in the Green Movement.

He jointly manages a public forest which involves taking an inventory of trees and birds, and cutting back undergrowth.

• He tries to find a way to actually "belong to the land." Turtle Island is the name for the North American continent based on many creation myths of the people who have been here for millennia. Snyder's vision is a rediscovery of this land and the ways "by which we might become natives of the place" by putting down roots, understanding plants and animals, knowing where our water comes from, and "ceasing to think and act as newcomers and invaders."

• He encourages us to see ourselves as interdependent energy fields of great potential wisdom and compassion. He challenges us to know our own nature; and to know our interconnectedness with one another and with all life, animate and inanimate. In his eyes reverence for life includes reverence for other species and future human lives.

• He exemplifies the position that to restore our faith in systems we need to adopt a systemic approach.

> ". . . it's not *in time* at all that we study our world and ourselves. There's no close or far. We have, simply, the chance to fill out the whole picture now, for the first time in human experience. It is beginning to be possible to look in one wide gaze at all that human beings have been and done on the whole planet, as one small part of the web of Gaia the earth-life-Goddess."[8]

APPENDIX F. A WHOLESOME ORGANIZATION

The Body Shop illustrates what can happen when the strengths of the five realities are incorporated into an organizational system. This manufacturing and retail business was founded by Anita Roddick in Brighton, England, in 1976. Specializing in hair and skin care, the company now boasts more than 1,400 shops in 46 countries. In the fiscal year ending February, 1996, The Body Shop posted worldwide retail sales of $906.1 million.

Although she did not intentionally use the ideas presented in this book, one reason for the success of Anita Roddick's enterprise may be that it exemplifies a wholesome organization. What follows is a review of how this organization combines the best of five worlds.

The "King of the Mountain" reality is apparent in Roddick's attention to image which she believes is as important as her products. In order to remain true to her original concept she has made certain that all of the shops have a common look, feel, and smell. The shops are painted dark green and are set up in a similar manner. The number and kinds of products displayed is strictly controlled. There is an effort to retain a distinctive "corporate aroma" through the products. Those who work in the shops are similar in age and appearance. (Over 75% of the staff members are women under the age of 30.)

The organization is a model of centralized authority. Calling her organization "paternalistic and caring," Roddick retains the right to determine the agreement under which the franchises operate. All of the franchise owners are expected to comply with directives from the corporate office. Failure to conform to this agreement can lead to closure. She and the district managers visit the shops regularly to ensure compliance.

There are five layers that form a hierarchy: the founders, senior executives, department heads, managers, and staff members (those who work in the shops, in the production sections, and in the shipping departments.) An infrastructure in the form of an eleven point charter of "Feel-Good Commandments" provides direction on how to keep records and how to approach customers.

The product line is simple and specialized. Roddick searches for precedents from around the world, relying on ingredients with a history of safety. Then she replicates existing substances. Every product is thoroughly researched and tested before it is adopted. Attention to detail is apparent in the labels that list all of the contents of each product.

"Motocross" elements are evident in the firm's roots. Roddick started the business because she needed to survive, financially. She began with a "World War II" mentality that meant saving, scrimping, and avoiding waste. Based on her extensive experience operating other businesses prior to opening The Body Shop, Roddick sees herself as a trader.

Basic to Roddick's success is knowing what features set her apart from the competition, then leveraging these to her advantage. She exploits novelty in both her methods and products. She knows how to gain market share through media exposure. She knows the market she's in and doesn't attempt to diversify.

All of the Body Shop's leaders are hard drivers, motivators, trouble-shooters, and trail blazers. Roddick keeps a very busy schedule traveling, looking for new products, and exploring new causes. She loves challenges. She claims a key to her success is setting a new direction and pace by going in the opposite direction to everyone else. Part of her role is to ignite a flame and mobilize zeal through personal visits and media presentations. Area managers are available to solve problems and respond to the need for quick fixes.

A "White Water Rafting" reality is recognizable in Roddick's view of business as a system of trade in which money is exchanged for products, services, and information. The company is a network of small, inter-linked ventures. The franchise owners are self-managed. They encourage self-service as a way to convey the company's endorsement of non-manipulative and non-exploitative approaches.

Employees are trained to create an atmosphere where customers matter. Customer orientation is demonstrated by offering choices of as little or as much of the available products as customers need and want. Customers and employees can find out anything they want to know about the way the company does business. Customers are encouraged to give feedback by sending letters and putting ideas into suggestion boxes.

Using multiple avenues, Roddick makes an effort to ensure effective communication. She produces documentaries through her own video company. Employees receive newsletters and view the multi-lingual video show, "Talking Shop," on a weekly basis. There are informational displays throughout all of the offices and warehouses. She uses charts, photographs, quotations, anecdotes, pamphlets, and rumors to get the word out. Delivery trucks serve as moving billboards. The shops are intended to serve as centers of education and communication.

Anita Roddick believes it's just as important to train for knowledge as it is to train for a sale. Asserting that information is power, she introduced a school where shopkeepers learn about products, other cultures, social problems, environmental issues, and nature. Employees are helped to realize their potential through courses that cover interpersonal dynamics and human development.

The owners are dedicated to continuous improvement. They constantly upgrade the quality of the items they sell and the way the products are presented.

Elements of "The Magical Mystery Mime Troupe and Jazz Band" reality can be seen in the whimsical, enticing appearance of the shops. Company-wide events are designed to generate enthusiasm and passion. Customers and employees are encouraged to regard business as fun, to embrace joy and excitement, and to celebrate life. Anita Roddick personifies what it means to live life to the fullest by "being somebody and being remarkable."

The firm's vision is to improve the human condition by selling well-being. This vision is supported by a "Banner of Values." A central value is to establish trust by working in an honorable way. The founders believe that work should "enable the human spirit" and "make people feel better."

The entire organization is looked upon as a working community based on direct relationships between people. Loyalty and commitment stem from a feeling of connection to one another. The founders endeavor to create a sense of holism and spiritual development through love and care. They believe "work can open the doors to the heart."

Roddick believes that service is fundamental to what life is all about. She says it is immoral to trade on fear, to deceive customers, and to make women feel dissatisfied with the way they look. Among her core beliefs is "you forsake values at the cost of forsaking your workforce." By trading ethically and marketing products on the basis of trust she has established a high degree of credibility.

Based on the assertion that "business can have a human face," Roddick strives to be altruistic while making a profit. Her philosophy includes the idea that business should be a "partnership of profits with principles." Every shop takes on a special project that reflects the needs of that community. Employees are encouraged to be good citizens by participating in these projects on company time.

Another basic tenet in Roddick's approach is her commitment to "fly the flag of social change." She believes businesses should do more than make money and sell good products. Leaders should use the resources of business to solve major social problems. The Body Shop launches an international campaign every year that addresses issues of human rights such as AIDs, amnesty for political prisoners, and the repression of dissidents.

The "Dance With Gaia" reality is demonstrated in the company's worldwide focus and its emphasis on the planet as a global family. The founders seek ways to help people in developing countries find work by organizing community projects to make products from natural resources.

A community in Nepal produces handmade paper using banana and rice fiber. People in Mexico use maguey plants to make body scrub mitts. Nut oil is used to make hair products in Brazil. Native Americans in the U.S. raise blue corn for a line of skin products.

Roddick emphasizes the importance of gaining first-hand experience of cultures around the world. A job-swap program makes it possible for employees to exchange positions with shopkeepers in other countries.

Espousing "corporate activism," Roddick maintains that businesses should give something back to society. One example of how she practices what she preaches is a soap factory The Body Shop built in Glasgow, Scotland, to provide jobs for the unemployed.

Concern for the well-being of developing countries is borne out in a policy of "trade not aid." Roddick wants to establish relationships based on equality with members of third world countries. Her approach includes paying first world prices to these suppliers. In addition, she returns funds to the producing communities. Over 20% of the profits made from the sale of products that originate in these countries goes to services such as mass inoculation, cataract surgery, and food.

Roddick is a "passionate environmentalist." Each year she mounts an international campaign focused on an environmental issue such as saving the whales, stopping the burning of rain forests, and preventing acid rain.

An environmental projects department ensures compliance with the company's own standards for social responsibility. In the annual environmental statement the firm publicly discloses the results of an audit that follows the framework of the European Union Eco-Management and Audit Regulation. The waste management policy includes reducing, reusing, and recycling waste. The shops are living systems designed to unite green consumers.

The corporate policies and procedures attest to Roddick's respect for the natural world. The company stands firmly opposed to animal testing. Company cars run on lead-free gasoline. Employees are encouraged to use public transportation, ride bikes, or walk to work. Replentishable ingredients, recycled paper, and refillable containers are used throughout the organization. All of the products are biodegradable. Roddick employs close-to-source substances, searches for natural products from diverse cultures, and looks to nature for inspiration.

END NOTES

1. Lamott, A. (1994). *Bird by Bird*. New York: Doubleday, p. 44.

2. Høeg, P. (1993). *Borderliners*. New York: Dell, p. 37.

3. Chetwynd, T. (1972). *Dictionary for Dreamers*. Frogmore, St. Albans, U.K.: Paladin.

4. Brezsny, R. (1994, February 24-March 2). Real Astrology. *Metro*, p. 71.

5. Snyder, G. (1960). *Myths and Texts*. New York: New Directions, p. viii.

6. Snyder, G. (1974). *Turtle Island*. New York: New Directions, p. 98.

7. Snyder, G. (1974). *Turtle Island*. New York: New Directions, p. 107.

8. Snyder, G. (1960). *Myths & Texts*. New York: New Directions, p. viii.

GLOSSARY

Administrivia: details that derive from the administration of large organizations through departments and subdivisions managed by sets of officials who insist on rules and forms

Alternative system: a nontraditional system; In this book, "King of the Mountain" and "Motocross" represent traditional systems. "White Water Rafting," "Magical Mystery Mime Troupe and Jazz Band," and "Dance With Gaia" depict alternative systems.

Assumption: something that is taken for granted; a supposition

Atrophy: failure to grow due to lack of nourishment; a wasting away

Biosphere: the planetary system consisting of exposed continents, oceans, and the atmosphere

Both-and perspective: simultaneously looking at something from different points of view

Brainstorm: to engage in a group problem-solving technique that involves the spontaneous contribution of ideas from all members of the group.

Bureausis: organizational stagnation that derives from governmental officiousness, rigid rules, and inflexible routines

Capability: mental power; intelligence; understanding

Chaos: a state of confusion in which matter and space lack traditional form, order and predictability; a condition where things appear to be beyond control

Co-evolution: a mutually advantageous process whereby two or more entities gradually grow, unfold, and develop

Congruent: agreeing; corresponding; harmonious; a condition in which two or more entities coincide

Creeping inertia: gradual development of a condition whereby one is disinclined to move or act, preferring instead to remain in a fixed condition

Cross-pollination: the interchange or interaction of different ideas and cultures, especially of a broadening nature

Dialogue: a mode of exchange in which the participants fully appreciate each other as genuine beings and pay attention to the processes that take place during conversation

Dualism: the theological doctrine that two radically independent elements are present within man (the spiritual and the physical), and that these represent two natures (good and bad); in this book the term refers to the perception of reality in terms of polarities which results in separations between mind and matter, subject and object, and the knower and the known

Ecosystem: a unit of living entities together with their environment

Emotional acre: A friend of Ann Lamott's shared with her the idea that each of us is born with an emotional acre. It is ours to use as we please as long as we don't hurt other people. If someone comes onto this acre and tries to control it, we have the right to ask that person to leave. (See "End Notes.")

Either/or perspective: polarized thinking based on dualism
End user: someone who uses a computer
Entity: a thing that has a real and individual existence

Feedback: the return of information to the source of a process or action for the purpose of control or correction; the information so transmitted
Flame: to attack other end users
Flak-catcher: A mid-level bureaucrat who is responsible for handling complaints, ~ solving problems, and shielding superiors
Flexer: someone who is pliant and able to bend; one who adapts and accommodates; one who is not rigid or obstinate
Friend of Gaia: an ecologically-oriented individual who works for the good of the planet
Fusion: a union of different things through melting

Gaia: Greek for "Earth Goddess"
Gaia consciousness: perceiving the Earth as a living entity; appreciating that everything on the Earth is alive and connected; considering the long-term ramifications of present-day actions
Gaia Hypothesis: the view that the Earth itself is a living system; James Lovelock and others postulate that the biosphere maintains stability and keeps the planet healthy by controlling the chemical and physical environment; this process is self-regulating
Groupthink: conformity to group values, ethics, and world view

Holistic: emphasizing the organic or functional relation between parts and wholes.

In-group: a collection of individuals who share a sense of solidarity by virtue of their position power and/or their political acumen

Junkie: one who is addicted to someone or something
Junk mail: E-mail messages unrelated to business issues

"KISS" admonition: a warning to "Keep it simple, stupid"

Life force: the peculiarity that distinguishes the living from the nonliving; vitality; physical or mental vigor
Lifestyle: a way of life

Manifest: to make clear or evident; to show plainly; to reveal; to prove
Matchmaker: someone who arranges connections for others
Metamorphosis: change of form, shape, structure, or substance; a marked or complete change of character, appearance, or condition
Metaphor: a figure of speech in which one thing is likened to a different thing, by being spoken of as if it were that different thing
Metaphysical: beyond the physical or material; incorporeal, supernatural, or transcendental

Nationalism: devotion to the interests or culture of one particular nation
Nepotism: the practice of appointing relatives to profitable positions, in disregard of the claims of others better fitted for the offices

Network: a collection of people who share interests in common; individuals dedicated to a common purpose who act in concert to bring about some type of change

Newbies: inexperienced end users of computers

Node: a central point of concentration; in a computer network, an individual who is linked electronically to others

Office politics: the practice of relating to others on the basis of manipulative tactics; key considerations include: submitting to authority, playing it safe, self-interest, and communicating indirectly

Organic: of, having the characteristics of, or derived from living organisms

Organism: a complex structure of interdependent and subordinate elements whose relations and properties are largely determined by their function in the whole.

Organization: any unified, consolidated group of elements; a systematized whole, especially a body of people brought into being for some specific purpose; the administrative structure of a business

Paradigm: a pattern, example, or model; a belief or explanation of observed phenomena that is shared by a community of people; what human beings believe about the way things are; a world view or superstructure that explains what one has observed; a framework of thought or a schema for understanding and explaining certain aspects of reality

Paradigm shift: a new knowing and a distinctly different way of thinking that, due to its larger perspective, transforms traditional knowledge and reconciles apparent contradictions; occurs when an individual or an organization finds itself "out of fit" with many aspects of its internal and external environment; may be an overlap of old and new, a case where the new is superimposed on the old, or a complete transformation

Paradox: a statement that seems contradictory, unbelievable, or absurd, but that may actually be true in fact

Paternalism: the principle or system of governing or controlling a country, group of employees, etc. in a manner suggesting a father's relationship with his children

Polymorph: an entity that passes through several or various forms

Risk addiction: habitual inclination to expose oneself to the chance of danger, peril, jeopardy, hazard, injury, or loss

Risk-aversion: to be reluctant or unwilling to expose oneself to danger

Risk-embracing: to welcome and readily accept the chance of danger

Ritual: a set form or system of rites

Robust: having strength or vigorous health; in this book: having the ability to assume all five shapes

Sandbox: in this book, the term refers to work organizations that are closed, rigid, and resistant to change; they embrace an either/or perspective and tend to expel dissidents

Schmoozing: to spend time talking with other people

Self: the identity, character, individuality, or essential qualities of a given person; one's own person as distinct from all others

The seventh generation: children who will be born seven generations from now

Shaman: a wizard, conjurer, teacher, and healer

Shape: form; capacity; a set of capabilities

Shapeshift: to alter one's makeup or identifying features; to change one's perspective and behavior

Shrink-to-fit: to force one's self to become smaller, psychologically, in order to fit a given form; the term derives from shrink-wrap, a tough clear plastic film that forms a tightly fitting package when heated

Sustainable society: a society in which people are dedicated to putting back what they take out; it includes commitment to the practice of meeting the needs of the present without compromising the ability of future generations to meet their needs; it involves using renewable resources while conserving natural resources where renewable options are not available

System: a method of classification; a regular, orderly way of doing something; a set of facts, principles, rules, etc. classified or arranged in a regular, orderly form so as to show a logical plan linking the various parts; a set or arrangement of things so related or connected as to form a unity or whole; the world or universe; an abstract model that defines a set of elements and identifies the relations among these elements; a set of elements that hang together because they continually affect each other and operate toward a common purpose

Systematic: made or arranged according to a plan; methodical; regular; orderly

Systemic: of or pertaining to a system

Systems thinking: a method of focusing on the quality of relationships among entities rather than on specific characteristics of the elements that comprise them; looking at the interrelatedness of forces and seeing them as parts of a common process

Transformation: a new way of seeing; a change in human consciousness

Wholesome: sound in body, mind, and spirit; in this book the term refers to an organizational system that possesses attributes of all five stories

BIBLIOGRAPHY

Abbey, E. (1975). *The Monkey Wrench Gang*. New York: Avon.

Abbott, E. A. (1952). *Flatland*. New York: Dover.

Ackoff, R. L. & Emery, F. E. (1972). *On Purposive Systems*. Chicago: Aldine.

Adams, J. L. (1986). *Conceptual Blockbusting*. Reading, MA: Addison-Wesley.

Allen, P. G. (1992). *The Sacred Hoop*. Boston: Beacon.

Antolovich, G. (1994, September/October). Treating the Criminal Thinker. *New Times*, 1(3), 1, 5.

Argyris, C. (1977, September/October). Double Loop Learning in Organizations. *Harvard Business Review*, 115-125.

Argyris, C. (1990). *Overcoming Organizational Defenses*. Boston: Allyn & Bacon.

Argyris, C. (1991, May/June). Teaching Smart People How to Learn. *Harvard Business Review*, 99-109.

Aronson, E. (1980). *The Social Animal*. San Francisco: W. H. Freeman.

Arrien, A. (1996, January). Bringing in the Blessing Way. *Heart Dance Magazine*, 66, pp. 24, 27.

Arrien, A. (1993). *The Four Fold Way: Walking the Paths of the Warrior, Teacher, Healer, and Visionary*. San Francisco: Harper.

Arrien, A. (1992). *Signs of Life: The Five Universal Shapes and How to Use Them*. Sonoma, CA: Arcus.

Ashkenas, R., Ulrich, D., Jick, T., & Kerr, S. (1995). *The Boundaryless Organization*. San Francisco: Jossey-Bass.

Atwood, M. (1993). *The Robber Bride*. New York: Doubleday.

Austen, H. I. (1990). *The Heart of the Goddess*. Berkeley: Wingbow.

Awiakta, M. (1978). *Abiding Appalachia: Where Mountain and Atom Meet*. Memphis, TN: St Luke's.

Awiakta, M. (1993). *Selu: Seeking the Corn-Mother's Wisdom*. Golden, CO: Fulcrum.

Baltzell, E. D. (Ed.) (1968). *The Search for Community in Modern America*. New York: Harper & Row.

Banathy, B. H. (1973). *Developing a Systems View of Education*. Seaside, CA: Intersystems.

Banathy, B. H. (1968). *Instructional Systems*. Palo Alto, CA: Fearon.

Banathy, B. H. (1986, October 13-17). "A Systems View of Development." Budapest: UNESCO.

Barati, A. (1965). *The Tantric Tradition*. Garden City, NJ: Anchor.

Bates, K. L. (Ed.) (1921). *Once Upon a Time: A Book of Old-Time Fairy Tales*. Chicago: Rand McNally.

Bateson, G. (1972). *Steps to an Ecology of Mind*. New York: Ballantine.

Beer, M., Eisenstat, R. A., & Spector, B. (1990, November/ December). Why Change Programs Don't Produce Change. *Harvard Business Review*, 158-166.

Bennis, W. G. & Slater, P. E. (1968). *The Temporary Society*. New York: Harper & Row.

Benson, H. (1987). *Your Maximum Mind*. New York: Random.

Benton, L. R. (1970, March). The Many Faces of Conflict: How Differences in Perception Cause Differences of Opinion. *Supervisory Management*, 7-10.

Berman, M. (1989). *Coming to Our Senses*. New York: Bantam.

Berman, M. (1981). *The Reenchantment of the World*. Ithaca, NY: Cornell University Press.

Bernhard, Y. (1975). *Self-Care*. Millbrae, CA: Celestial Arts.

Bettelheim, B. (1977). *The Uses of Enchantment: The Meaning and Importance of Fairy Tales*. New York: Vintage.

Block, P. (1987). *The Empowered Manager*. San Francisco: Jossey-Bass.

Blumenthal, B. & Haspeslagh, P. (1994, Spring). Toward a Definition of Corporate Transformation. *Sloan Management Review*, 101-106.

The Body Shop 1996 Annual Report and Accounts. West Sussex, U.K.: The Body Shop International.

Bohm, D. (1985). *Unfolding Meaning*. London: Routledge & Kegan Paul.

Bolen, J. S. (1984). *Goddesses in Every Woman*. New York: HarperCollins.

Bolen, J. S. (1979) *The Tao of Psychology: Synchronicity and the Self*. San Francisco: Harper & Row.

Bolman, L. G. & Deal, T. E. (1991). *Reframing Organizations: Artistry, Choice and Leadership*. San Francisco: Jossey-Bass.

Boorstin, D. J. (1961). *The Image, or What Happened to the American Dream*. New York: Random.

Bowes, P. (1976). *The Hindu Religious Tradition: A Philosophical Approach*. London: Routledge & Kegan Paul.

Bradford, D. L. & Cohen, A. R. (1984, January). The Postheroic Leader. *Training and Development Journal*, 40-49.

Bradley, M. Z. (1982). *The Mists of Avalon*. New York: Ballantine.

Brezsny, R. (1994, February 24-March 2). Real Astrology. *Metro*, p. 71.

Briggs, J. & Peat, F. D. (1989). *The Turbulent Mirror*. New York: Harper & Row.

Broadersen, E. (1995, October). Chaos in Arcadia. *American Conservatory Stagebill*, 20-25.

Brown, J. (1990, January). Elements of New Paradigm Consulting. *World Business Academy Perspectives*, 2, 5-8.

Brown, L. D. (1972). Research Action: Organizational Feedback, Understanding and Change. *Journal of Applied Behavioral Science*, 8(6), 697-711.

Buber, M. (1970). *I and Thou*. (W. Kaufmann, Trans.) New York: Charles Scribner's Sons.

Burdman, P. (1996, March 10). Robert Thurman. *San Francisco Examiner & Chronicle*, p. 3.

Burlingham, B. (1990-91, Winter). More Than Skin Deep. *The Best of Business Quarterly*, 39-47.

Burroughs, R. (1991, February). Systems Thinking in Tucson. *Electronic Learning*, 12-13.

Caldecott, M. (1988). *Women in Celtic Myth*. Rochester, VT: Destiny.

Callenbach, E. (1977). *Ecotopia*. New York: Bantam.

Callenbach, E., Capra, F., Goldman, L., Lutz, R., & Marburg, S. (1993). *EcoManagement*. San Francisco: Berrett-Koehler.

Campbell, J. (1968). *Masks of God: Creative Mythology*. New York: Viking.

Campbell, J. (1972). *Myths to Live By*. New York: Viking.

Capacchione, L. (1988). *The Power of Your Other Hand*. North Hollywood, CA: Newcastle.

Capra, F. (1975). *The Tao of Physics*. Berkeley: Shambhala.

Capra, F. (1982). *The Turning Point*. New York: Bantam.

Cavaleri, S. & Obloj, K. (1993). *Management Systems: A Global Perspective*. Belmont, CA: Wadsworth.

Chapman, G. (1996, February 26). Longing to Return to '50s Grows From High-Tech Turmoil. *San Jose Mercury News*, p. 3E.

Charan, R. (1991, September/October). How Networks Reshape Organizations-For Results. *Harvard Business Review*, 104-115.

Charlesworth, K. & Gribbin, J. (1990). *The Cartoon History of Time*. New York: Penguin.

Checkland, P. (1981). *Systems Thinking, Systems Practice.* New York: Wiley.

Chetwynd, T. (1972). *Dictionary for Dreamers.* Frogmore, St. Albans, U.K.: Paladin.

Chinen, A. B. (1992). *Once Upon a Midlife.* Los Angeles: Tarcher.

Chipongian, A.C. (1992, October 21). "Green" Cosmetics Mogul Speaks at the Graduate School of Business. *Stanford University Campus Report, 25*(3), 1.

Christ, C. P. (1987). *Laughter of Aphrodite.* San Francisco: Harper.

Churchman, C. W. (1983). (Rev.) *The Systems Approach.* New York: Dell.

Churchman, C. W. (1979). *The Systems Approach and Its Enemies.* New York: Basic Books.

Clark, T. (1996, September 1). Gary Snyder Tells the Tale of the Tribe. *San Francisco Sunday Examiner & Chronicle: Book Review, pp. 1, 10.*

Clay, J. (1996, January-February). The Diversity Debate: Counterpoint. *Utne Reader,* pp. 36-37.

Collingwood, R. G. (1945). *The Idea of Nature.* London: Oxford University.

Collins, G. (1992, May 24). Think Point A Leads to Point B? *San Jose Mercury News: West Supplement,* pp. 6-7.

Combs, A. & Holland, M. (1990). *Synchronicity: Science, Myth, and the Trickster.* New York: Paragon.

Cose, E. (1993, November 15). Rage of the Privileged. *Newsweek,* 56-59, 61-63.

Cox, T. H. & Blake, S. (1991, August). Managing Cultural Diversity: Implications for Organizational Competitiveness. *Academy of Management Executive, 5*(3), 45-56.

Crowther, R. L. (1986). *Women/Nature/Destiny: Female/Male Equity for Global Survival.* Denver: Directions.

Cummings, T. (1980). *Systems Theory for Organization Development.* New York: Wiley.

Dahlke, R. (1992). *Mandalas of the World.* New York: Sterling.

Daly, M. (1973). *Beyond God the Father.* Boston: Beacon.

Davenport, T. H. (1994, March/April). Saving IT's Soul: Human-Centered Information Management. *Harvard Business Review,* 119-132.

Davis, P. J. & Hersh, R. (1987). *Descartes Dream: The World According to Mathematics.* Boston: Houghton Mifflin.

Davis, S. M. (1987). *Futureperfect.* Reading, MA: Addison-Wesley.

de Geus, A. P. (1988, March-April). Planning as Learning. *Harvard Business Review,* 70-74.

Deming, W. E. (1993). *The New Economics.* Cambridge: MA: Massachusetts Institute of Technology.

DeVinne, P. M. (Ed.) (1987). *American Heritage Illustrated Encyclopedic Dictionary.* Boston: Houghton Mifflin.

Dinnerstein, D. (1976). *The Mermaid and the Minotaur.* New York: Harper & Row.

Dixey, R. (1990, Summer). Scientific Analysis and the Recovery of the Natural World. *Noetic Sciences Review,* 7-13, 33-38.

Doktor, R. H. (1990, Winter). Asian and American CEOs: A Comparative Study. *Organizational Dynamics,* 46-56.

Donnelly, K. (1995, November 15). Fascinating Rhythms. *San Jose Mercury News,* pp. 1E, 8E.

Dourley, J. P. (1981). *The Psyche as Sacrament: A Comparative Study of C.G. Jung and Paul Tillich.* Toronto, Canada: Inner City.

Drucker, P. F. (1988, January/February). The Coming of the New Organization. *Harvard Business Review,* 45-53.

Dumaine, B. (1991, June 17). The Bureaucracy Busters. *Fortune,* 36-42, 46, 50.

Duvoisin, R. (1943). *Fairy Tales from Switzerland.* London: Frederick Muller.

Edidin, P. (1989, May). Follow Your Bliss. *Psychology Today,* 62-64.

Eisler, R. (1987). *The Chalice and the Blade.* San Francisco: Harper & Row.

Eisler, R. (1995). *Sex, Myth and the Politics of the Body.* San Francisco: HarperCollins.

Eisler, R. & Loye, D. (1990). *The Partnership Way.* New York: HarperCollins.

Emery, F. E. (1967). The Next Thirty Years: Concepts, Methods and Anticipations. *Human Relations, 20*(3), 199-237.

Emery, F. E. (Ed.) (1969). *Systems Thinking.* Harmondsworth: Penguin.

Emery, F. E. & Thorsrud, E. (1964). *Form and Content in Industrial Democracy.* Oslo: Oslo University Press.

Emery, F. E. & Trist, E. L. (1973). *Towards a Social Ecology: Appreciation of the Future in the Present.* New York:Plenum.

Estes, C. P. (1992). *Women Who Run with the Wolves.* New York: Ballantine.

Etzioni, A. (1968). *The Active Society: A Theory of Societal and Political Processes.* New York: Free Press.

Etzioni, A. (1993). *The Spirit of Community.* New York: Crown.

Ewing, D. W. (1983). *Do It My Way or You're Fired!* New York: Wiley.

Fabian, J. (1990). *Creative Thinking and Problem Solving.*Chelsea, MI: Lewis.

Fauteck, L. (1995, May & June). The Artist as Shaman. *Open Exchange,* p. 36.

Feldman, R. H. (1996, October 20). A Nation's Dreams Wilt on the Edge of the Desert (A Review of *Don't Call It Night* by Amos Oz.) *San Francisco Sunday Examiner and Chronicle Book Review,* p. 4.

Ferguson, M. (1980). *The Aquarian Conspiracy: Personal and Social Transformation in the 1980s.* Los Angeles: Tarcher.

Field, M. & Golubitsky, M. (1992). *Symmetry in Chaos: A Search for Pattern in Mathematics, Art, and Nature.* New York: Oxford University.

Finkel, C. (1984, April). Where Learning Happens. *Training and Development Journal.* 32-36.

Fisher, A. B. (1992, September 21). When Will Women Get to the Top? *Fortune,* 44-48, 52, 56.

Flinn, J. (1995, October 15). Pristine Chapels. *San Francisco Examiner Magazine,* pp. 24, 48.

Flood, R. L. & Jackson, M. C. (1991). *Creative Problem Solving: Total Systems Intervention.* New York: Wiley.

Flood, R. L. & Carson, E. R. (1988). *Dealing with Complexity: An Introduction to the Theory and Application of Systems Science.* New York: Plenum.

Fordham, F. (1953). *An Introduction to Jung's Psychology.* Baltimore: Penguin.

Fox, M. & Swimme, B. (1982). *Manifesto! For a Global Civilization.* Santa Fe: Bear.

Fox, W. (1990). *Towards a Transpersonal Ecology.* Boston: Shambhala.

Frazer, J. G. (1922). *The Golden Bough.* New York: Collier.

Freedman, D. H. (1992, November-December). Is Management Still a Science? *Harvard Business Review,* 26-28, 30-35.

French, W. & Bell, C. (1984). *Organizational Development.* Englewood, Cliffs, NJ: Prentice Hall.

Friedlander, F. (1994). Toward Whole Systems and Whole People. *Organization Speaking Out, 1*(1), 59-64.

Fritz, R. (1991). *Creating.* New York: Fawcett Columbine.

Fritz, R. (1984). *The Path of Least Resistance.* New York: Fawcett Columbine.

Gabor, A. (1992, February 9). Some Firms Scrap the Star System. *San Jose Mercury News,* p. 1PC.

Gadon, E. W. (1989). *The Once and Future Goddess: A Symbol for Our Time.* San Francisco: Harper & Row.

Gaffney, R. (1984-1985, Winter-Spring) Systems Thinking in Business: An Interview with Peter Senge. *Revision, 7*(2), 56-63.

Gardner, B. H. & Demello, S. (1993, July-August). Systems Thinking in Action. *Healthcare Forum Journal,* 25-28.

Garud, R. & Kotha, S. (1994, October). Using the Brain as a Metaphor to Model Flexible Production Systems. *The Academy of Management Review, 19*(4), 671-697.

Garvin, D. A. (1993, July/August). Building a Learning Organization. *Harvard Business Review*, 78-91.

Gawain, S. (1995, Fall). The Journey Toward Wholeness. *Open Exchange*, p. 91.

Gelbspan, R. (1995, December 17). The Heat is On. *San Jose Mercury News*, pp. 1P, 4P.

Gersick, C. J. G. (1991, January). Revolutionary Change Theories: A Multilevel Exploration of the Punctuated Equilibrium Paradigm. *The Academy of Management Review*, 16(1), 10-35.

Gettlin, R. (1994, April 10). A Different Kind of House. *San Jose Mercury News: Parade Magazine*, pp. 24-25.

Gibran, K. (1957). *The Prophet*. New York: Knopf.

Gilchrist, E. (1989). *Light Can Be Both Wave and Particle*. Boston: Little, Brown.

Gilder, G. (1989, August 28). The World's Next Source of Wealth. *Fortune*, 116-120.

Giles, M. E. (1982). *The Feminist Mystic*. New York: Crossroad.

Gill, S. D. & Sullivan, I. F. (1988). *Dictionary of Native American Mythology*. New York: Oxford University Press.

Gilligan, C. (1982). *In a Different Voice*. Cambridge, MA: Harvard University Press.

Ginsberg, A. (1993). *Snapshot Poetics*. San Francisco: Chronicle.

Gleick, J. (1987). *Chaos*. New York: Viking.

Glenn, J. (1996, January-February). The Nitty-Gritty of Nirvana. *Utne Reader*, pp. 91-99.

Goldberg, N. (1986). *Writing Down the Bones: Freeing the Writer Within*. Boston: Shambhala.

Goodman, P. S. (1979). *Assessing Organizational Change: The Rushton Quality of Work Experiment*. New York: Wiley.

Gould, J., DiBella, A., & Nevis, E. (1993, October). Organizations as Learning Systems. *The Systems Thinker*, 4(8), 1-4.

Gray, J. (1992). *Men Are from Mars; Women Are from Venus*. New York: HarperCollins.

Gribben, J. (1988). *The Omega Point: The Search for the Missing Mass and the Ultimate Fate of the Universe*. New York: Bantam.

Hamilton, E. (1942). *Mythology*. Boston: Little, Brown.

Hammer, M. (1992, August 31). Management's New Gurus. *Business Week*, 44-52.

Hampden-Turner, C. (1990). *Charting the Corporate Mind: Solutions to Business Conflicts*. Oxford, England: Blackwell.

Hampden-Turner, C. (1990). *Corporate Culture: From Vicious to Virtuous Circles*. London: Hutchinson.

Hampden-Turner, C. (1985, January). Is There a New Paradigm? Paper presented at the meeting of Shell International managers at the Shell Centre in London.

Hampden-Turner, C. (1981). *Maps of the Mind*. New York: Collier.

Hampden-Turner, C. (1989). The Quest for the Great White Whale or How Attempts to Tame a Living System Can Get You Deeper and Deeper Into Trouble. A Report to the Hanover Insurance Company on the New Jersey Automobile Full Insurance Underwriting Association. (Available from Hanover Metro Branch, 330 S. Randolphville Rd., Piscatawya, NJ 08855.)

Handy, C. (1989). *The Age of Unreason*. Boston: Harvard Business School.

Hanks, K. & Parry, J. A. (1983). *Wake Up Your Creative Genius*. Los Altos, CA: William Kaufmann.

Harding, M. E. (1965). *The "I" and the "Not-I."* Princeton, NJ: Princeton University.

Harding, M. E. (1974). *Psychic Energy: Its Source and Its Transformation*. Princeton, NJ: Princeton University.

Harding, M. E. (1970). *The Way of All Women*. New York: Harper & Row.

Harding, M. E. (1971). *Woman's Mysteries Ancient and Modern*. New York: Harper & Row.

Harris, C. (1994, July). Books Build Community. *The Price/ Costco Connection,* pp. BB1-BB2.

Harris, T. G. (1993, May/June). The Post-Capitalist Executive: An Interview with Peter F. Drucker. *Harvard Business Review,* 115-122.

Hart, A. D. (1993). *The Crazymaking Workplace.* Ann Arbor: Servant.

Hart, L. B. (1981). *Learning From Conflict.* Reading, MA: Addison-Wesley.

Harvey, A. (1991). *Hidden Journey.* New York: Arkana.

Harvey, J. B. & Albertson, D. R. (1971, September). Neurotic Organizations: Symptoms, Causes and Treatment. *Personnel Journal, 50*(9), 695-699.

Hawken, P. (1987) *The Ecology of Commerce.* New York: HarperCollins.

Hawken, P. (1987). *Growing a Business.* New York: Fireside.

Hawking, S. (1988). *A Brief History of Time.* New York: Bantam.

The Healing Place. (1996, February). *Outlook: Arts, Issues & Living From Mendocino,* (55), 14.

Henderson, H. (1981). *The Politics of the Solar Age.* New York: Doubleday.

Hillerman, T. (1986). *Skinwalkers.* New York: HarperCollins.

Hillman, A. (1994). *The Dancing Animal Woman.* Norfolk, CT: Bramble.

Høeg, P. (1993). *Borderliners.* New York: Dell.

Høeg, P. (1993). *Smilla's Sense of Snow.* New York: Farrar Straus Ciroux, p. 245.

Holt, P. (1996, February 4-10). Houses in Tune With the Earth. *San Francisco Chronicle Book Review,* pp. 1, 7.

Hopkins, T. J. (1971). *The Hindu Religious Tradition.* Encino, CA: Dickenson.

Hoshmand, L. L. S. T. (1989, January). Alternate Research Paradigms: A Review and Teaching Proposal. *The Counseling Psychologist, 17*(1), 3-79.

Hosking, D. M. & Anderson, N. R. (1992). *Organizational Change and Innovation: Psychological Perspectives and Practices in Europe.* London: Routledge.

Huff, A. S. (1990). *Mapping Strategic Thought.* New York: Wiley.

Hurst, D. K. (1984, May-June). Of Boxes, Bubbles, and Effective Management. *Harvard Business Review,* 78-88.

Hyatt, J. (1989, February). The Odyssey of an Excellent Man. *INC.,* 63-69.

Imai, M. (1986). *Kaizen.* New York: McGraw-Hill.

Iwata, E. (1996, August 4). Nirvana Corp. *The San Francisco Examiner,* D1, D4, D12.

Iyer, P. (1996, January-February). The Diversity Debate: Point. *Utne Reader,* pp. 35-36.

Jacobs, H. (1961). *Psychology and Hindu Sadhana.* London: Allen & Unwin.

Jamal, M. (1995). *Deerdancer: The Shapeshifter Archetype in Story and Trance.* New York: Arkana.

Jamal, M. (1987). *Shape Shifters: Shaman Women in Contemporary Society.* New York: Arkana.

Jantsch, E. (1980). *The Self-Organizing Universe.* New York: Pergamon.

Jones, R. S. (1982). *Physics as Metaphor.* Minneapolis, MN: University of Minnesota.

Joy, W. B. (1979). *Joy's Way.* Los Angeles: J. P. Tarcher.

Kanter, R. M. (1983). *The Changemasters.* New York: Simon & Schuster.

Kanter, R. M. (1972). *Commitment and Community.* Cambridge, MA: Harvard University.

Kanungo, R. N. & Conger, J. A. (1993, August). Promoting Altruism as a Corporate Goal. *The Academy of Management Executive, 7*(3), 37-48.

Kaplan, D. E. & Marshall, A. (1996, July). The Cult at the End of the World. *Wired,* 135-137, 176-184.

Kaswan, J. (1988). *Cooperative Democracy.* (Available from The Alternatives Center, 1740 Walnut St., Berkeley, CA 94709.)

Kaswan, J. and Kaswan, R. (1989, Spring). The Mondragon Cooperatives. *Whole Earth Review,* 8-17.

158   *Bibliography*

Kato, D. (1996, February 25). Layoff's Emotional Toll. *San Jose Mercury News,* pp. 1H, 5H.

Kauffman, D. L. (1980). *Systems One: An Introduction to Systems Thinking.* St. Paul, MN: Future Systems.

Kauffman, D. L. (1981). *Systems Two: Human Systems.* St. Paul, MN: Future Systems.

Keen, S. (1986). *Faces of the Enemy.* San Francisco: Harper & Row.

Keirsey, D. & Bates, M. (1984). *Please Understand Me.* Del Mar, CA: Prometheus Nemesis.

Kelley, K. W. (Ed.) (1988). *The Home Planet.* Reading, MA: Addison-Wesley.

Kelly, B. B. (1995, August 27). Art and Soul of a New Machine. *San Jose Mercury News, West Supplement,* pp. 12-13, 22-23.

Kelly, K. (1996, July). Anticipatory Democracy. *Wired,* 45-52, 187.

Kenneally, T. (1995, October 20). Real Life vs. the Internet. *BAM.* p. 9.

Kets de Vries, M. F. R. (1994, August). The Leadership Mystique. *Academy of Management Executive, 8*(3), 73-92.

Kets de Vries, M. F. R. & Miller, D. (1984). *The Neurotic Organization.* San Francisco: Jossey-Bass.

Kiefer, C. F. & Stroh, P. (1984). A New Paradigm for Developing Organizations. In J. D. Adams (Ed.), *Transforming Work.* Alexandria, VA: Miles River.

Kim, W. C. & Mauborgne, R. A. (1992, July-August). Parables of Leadership. *Harvard Business Review,* 123-128.

King, D. (1981, January/February). Three Cheers for Conflict! *Personnel,* 13-19.

King, S. K. (1990). *Urban Shaman.* New York: Simon & Schuster.

Koberg, D. & Bagnall, J. (1972). *The Universal Traveler: A Soft-Systems Guide to Creativity, Problem-Solving and the Process of Reaching Goals.* Los Altos, CA: William Kaufmann.

Kuhn, T. (1972). *The Structure of Scientific Revolutions.* (2nd ed.) Chicago: University of Chicago.

Lamott, A. (1994). *Bird by Bird.* New York: Anchor.

Land, G. & Jarman, B. (1992). *Breakpoint and Beyond.* New York: HarperCollins.

Lao-tzu. (1988). *Tao Te Ching.* (S. Mitchell, Trans.) New York: HarperCollins.

Lappe, F. M. & DuBois, P. M. (1994). *The Quickening of America.* San Francisco: Jossey-Bass.

Larson, E. (1988, July). Forever Young. *INC.,* 50-62.

Laszlo, E. (1994). *Vision 2020: Reordering Chaos for Global Survival.* Yverdon, Switzerland: Gordon & Breach.

The Learning Organization Made Plain. (1991, October). *Training and Development,* 37-44.

Lee, V. (1994, Fall). The Eternal Quest for the Grail: An Interview with Jean Shinoda Bolen. *Common Ground,* 81, pp. 148-150, 169, 175.

LeGuin, U. K. (1985). *Always Coming Home.* New York: Bantam.

LeGuin, U. K. (1968). *A Wizard of Earthsea.* New York: Bantam.

Leibovich, M. (1994, August 5). Palo Alto Duo Helps Others Do Good. *San Jose Mercury News: Peninsula Living,* pp. 3-4.

Lerner, M. (1994). *Jewish Renewal: A Path to Healing and Transformation.* New York: Putnam's Sons.

Lerner, M. (1986). *Surplus Powerlessness.* Oakland, CA: Institute for Labor & Mental Health.

LeShan, L. (1976). *Alternate Realities.* New York: Ballantine.

LeShan, L. (1992). *The Psychology of War.* Chicago: Noble.

Lewin, R. (1992). *Complexity: Life at the Edge of Chaos.* New York: Macmillan.

Lewis, D. & Greene, J. (1982). *Thinking Better.* New York: Rawson, Wade.

Lilly, John (1972). *The Center of the Cyclone.* New York: Bantam.

Lifton, R. J. (1993). *The Protean Self: Human Resilience in an Age of Fragmentation.* New York: Basic Books.

Lovelock, J. (1979). *Gaia: A New Look at Life on Earth.* Oxford, England: Oxford University.

Luke, H. M. (1981). *Woman, Earth and Spirit: The Feminine in Symbol and Myth.* New York: Crossroad.

Mackenzie, H. (1992, February 3). A Report From Space. *Maclean's, 70.*

MacKinnon, D. & Baldanza, J. (1989). *The Twelve Men Who Walked on the Moon Reflect on Their Flights, Their Lives, and the Future.* Washington, DC: Acropolis.

MacMillan, J. (1995, November). Remembering Me, Remembering You. *Psychic Reader,* p. 5.

Malone, M. S. (1988, November 6). Coins of the Realm. *San Jose Mercury News, West Supplement,* pp. 16-19, 30-37.

Malone, M. S. & Davidow, B. (1994, May 17-31). Welcome to the Age of Virtual Corporations. *Bay Area Computer Currents,* pp. 37-39.

Malvaux, J. (1996, March 10). Downsizing Finally in the Spotlight. *San Francisco Examiner & Chronicle,* p. D-2.

Mander, J. (1991). *In the Absence of the Sacred: The Future of Technology and the Survival of the Indian Nations.* San Francisco: Sierra Club.

Manson, G. (1995, November 5). A Blurred Global Vision. *San Francisco Examiner & Chronicle,* p. 10.

Margulies, N. & Raia, A. (1972). *Organizational Development: Values, Process and Technology.* New York: McGraw-Hill.

Martin, A. (1996, January-February). Why Get Married? *Utne Reader,* pp. 17-18.

Matsumoto, M. (1988). *The Unspoken Way.* Tokyo: Kodansha.

Matthews, J. (1991). *Taliesin: Shamanism and the Bardic Mysteries in Britain and Ireland.* London: Aquarian.

Matthews, C. & Matthews, J. (1994). *The Encyclopedia of Celtic Wisdom: The Celtic Shaman's Sourcebook.* Shaftesbury, Dorset, England: Books, Ltd.

Maturana, H. R. & Varela, F. J. (1980). *Autopoiesis and Cognition: The Realization of the Living.* Boston: Reidel.

McCamant, K. & Durrett, C. (1994). (2nd Ed.) *Cohousing: A Contemporary Approach to Housing Ourselves.* Berkeley, CA: Ten Speed Press.

McHugh, P. (1995, November 26). Tom Hayden. *San Francisco Examiner & Chronicle,* p. 3.

McLuhan, N. P. (1996, February 1-7). Care Fakers. *Metro,* pp. 20-21.

McKenna, R. (1991, December). New World Marketing. *Upside,* 59-66.

McWhinney, W. (1990). Fractals Cast No Shadows. *International Synergy Institute Journal, 9,* 9-20.

McWhinney, W. (1989, April). (Rev.) Of Paradigms and System Theories. Unpublished manuscript, The Fielding Institute, Santa Barbara, CA.

McWhinney, W. (1992). *Paths of Change.* Newbury, Park, CA: Sage.

McWhinney, W. (1982). *A Study Guide for Systems Praxis.* Unpublished Manuscript, The Fielding Institute, Santa Barbara, CA.

McWhinney, W., McCulley, E. S., Webber, J. B., Smith, D. M., & Novokowsky, B. J. (1993). *Creating Paths of Change.* Venice, CA: Enthusion.

Meadows, D. H. (1982, Summer). Whole Earth Models and Systems. *Co-Evolution Quarterly,* 98-108.

Meier, D. (1985, May). New Age Learning: From Linear to Geodesic. *Training and Development Journal,* 38-43.

Metzner, R. (1971). *Maps of Consciousness.* New York: Macmillan.

Miles, R. (1988). *The Women's History of the World.* New York: Harper & Row.

Miller, W. H. (1992, March 16). Metamorphosis in the Desert. *Industry Week,* 27-34.

Millman, D. (1980). *Way of the Peaceful Warrior.* Tiburon, CA: Kramer.

Minar, D. W. & Greer, S. (1969). *The Concept of Community.* Chicago: Aldine.

Miners, S. (Ed.) (1984). *A Spiritual Approach to Male/Female Relations.* Wheaton, IL: Theosophical Publishing House.

Mink, D., Schultz, J. P. & Mink, B. P. (1979). *Developing and Managing Open Organizations: A Model and Methods for Maximizing Organizational Potential.* Austin, TX: Learning Concepts.

Mitroff, I. I. & Linstone, H. A. (1993). *The Unbounded Mind.* New York: Oxford University Press.

Mitroff, I. I., Mason, R. O. & Pearson, C. M. (1994, May). Radical Surgery: What Will Tomorrow's Organizations Look Like? *Academy of Management Executive, 8*(2), 11-20.

Monane, J. H. (1967). *A Sociology of Human Systems.* New York: Appleton, Century, Crofts.

Montouri, A. & Conti, I. (1993). *From Power to Partnership.* San Francisco: Harper.

Mookerjee, A. & Khanna, M. (1977). *The Tantric Way.* Boston: New York Graphic Society.

Morgan, G. (1982). *Beyond Methods: Strategies for Social Research.* Beverly Hills, CA: Sage.

Morgan, G. (1982). Cybernetics and Organization Theory: Epistemology or Technique. *Human Relations, 35*(7), 521-537.

Morgan, G. (1986). *Images of Organizations.* Newbury Park, CA: Sage.

Morgan, M. (1991). *Mutant Message Down Under.* New York: HarperCollins.

Morris, B. (1995, September 18). Executive Women Confront Midlife Crisis. *Fortune,* 60-62, 65, 68, 72, 74, 78, 80, 84, 86.

Morrison, P., Morrison, P, and The Office of Charles and Ray Eames (1982). *Powers of Ten.* New York: Scientific American Library.

Muktananda (1971). *Play of Consciousness.* Fallsburg, NY: Syda Foundation.

Murdock, M. (1990). *The Heroine's Journey: Woman's Quest for Wholeness.* Boston: Shambhala.

Nadler, D. A., Mirvis, P. H. & Cammann, C. (1976). The Ongoing Feedback System: Experimenting with a New Management Tool. *Organizational Dynamics, 4,* 63-80.

Naess, A. (1989). *Ecology, Community, and Lifestyle.* New York: Cambridge University.

Naisbett, J. & Aburdene P. (1985). *Re-Inventing the Corporation.* New York: Warner.

Naranjo, C. (1973). *The Healing Journey: New Approaches to Consciousness.* New York: Pantheon.

Nash, P. (1968). *Models of Man.* New York: Wiley.

Neely, A. (1994, July 31). Networking Portrayed as a Way of Sharing. *San Jose Mercury News,* P. 18.

Newhauser, P. C. (1989, August). Tribal Warfare in Organizations. *Soundview Executive Book Summaries, 11*(8), 1-8.

Nichols, L. (1996, February). Shifty Paradigms. *Outlook: Arts, Issues and Living From Mendocino,* p. 27.

Nirenberg, J. (1993). *The Living Organization.* Homewood, IL: Business One Irwin.

Norwood, K. & Smith, K. (1994). *Rebuilding Community in America.* Berkeley, CA: Shared Living Resources.

O'Boyle, T. F. (1990, June 4). From Pyramid to Pancake. *The Wall Street Journal,* pp. R37-R38.

O'Brien, T. (1995, October 22). Be-Glitched, Bothered and Bewildered. *San Jose Mercury News, West Supplement,* pp. 8-10,12-13, 26.

O'Brien, T. (1995, November 5). No Jerks Allowed. *San Jose Mercury News, West Supplement,* pp. 8-14, 25-26.

O'Connor, E. (1968). *Journey Inward, Journey Outward.* New York: Harper & Row.

O'Connor, E. (1971). *Our Many Selves.* New York: Harper & Row.

O'Connor, P. (1985). *Understanding Jung: Understanding Yourself.* New York: Paulist.

Ornstein, R. E. (1977). *The Psychology of Consciousness.* New York: Harcourt Brace Jovanovich.

Osborn, S. M. (1992, December 21). Companies Will Have to Get Smarter to Overcome Perennial Problems. *The San Jose Business Journal Special Report,* p. 23.

Osborn, S. M. (1992, December). Fielding as Corporate Consultant. *Fielding Magazine,* 17-18.

Osborn, S. M. (1994, November/December). Leaders as Boundary Spanners. *The New Leaders,* 5.

Osborn, S. M. (1992, July/August). The New Science of Leadership. *The New Leaders,* 5-6.

Osborn, S. M. (1990). *Performance Management: Paradigm Shift as a Factor in Diffusion of the Socio-Technical Systems Approach.* Unpublished doctoral dissertation, The Fielding Institute, Santa Barbara, CA.

Ouchi, W. G. (1980). Markets, Bureaucracies and Clans. *Administrative Science Quarterly, 25,* 10.

Pagels, E. (1979). *The Gnostic Gospels.* New York: Vintage.

Pagels, H. (1988). *Dreams of Reason: The Computer and the Rise of the Sciences of Complexity.* New York: Bantam.

Papp, P. (1983). *The Process of Change.* New York: Guilford.

Pascarella, P. (1986, January 6). The New Science of Management. *Industry Week, 45,* 47-48, 50.

Pava, C. (1983). *Managing New Office Technology: An Organizational Strategy.* New York: Free Press.

Perry, B. (1984). *Enfield: A High Performance System.* Bedford, MA: Digital Equipment Corporation.

Peters, T. J. (1992, December 28). Awards Go to Firms, People Who Had Nerve, Shook Things Up. *San Jose Mercury News,* p. 3C.

Peters, T. J. (1992). *Liberation Management: Necessary Disorganization for the Nanosecond Nineties.* New York: Knopf.

Peters, T. J. (1994, August 8). Quickly Eliminating Hierarchies Could Make Your Firm a Leader. *San Jose Mercury News,* p. 3D.

Peters, T. J. (1987). *Thriving on Chaos.* New York: Knopf.

Peters, T. J. (1993, July 19). "Whole" Truths Help Businesses Gauge Overall Performance. *San Jose Mercury News,* p. 9D.

Peters, T. J. & Waterman, R. H. (1982). *In Search of Excellence.* New York: Harper & Row.

Piercy, M. (1976). *Woman on the Edge of Time.* New York: Fawcett Crest.

Plant, J. (1989). *Healing the Wounds: The Promise of Ecofeminism.* Philadelphia: New Society.

Plotnikoff, D. (1994, July 23). It's a Beautiful Day in the Cyberhood. *San Jose Mercury News,* pp. 1C, 6C.

Presley, S. (1996, March-April). Be Less Vulnerable to Influence and Authority. *Open Exchange,* p. 18.

Preston, P. & Hawkins, B. L. (1979, November). Creative Conflict Management. *Supervisory Management,* 7-11.

Prigogine, I. & Stengers, I. (1984). *Order Out of Chaos.* New York: Bantam.

Progoff, I. (1973). *Jung, Synchronicity, and Human Destiny.* New York: Crown.

Quinn, J. B. (1996, February 26). Wages, Not Economic Indicators, Fuel the Fire Under Voters' Feet. *San Jose Mercury News,* p. 3E.

Quinn, R. E. (1988). *Beyond Rational Management.* San Francisco: Jossey-Bass.

Rader, D. (1988, April 24). The Town That Saved Itself. *San Jose Mercury News: Parade Magazine,* pp. 8-10.

Ray, M. & Rinzler, A. (Eds.) (1993). *The New Paradigm in Business.* Los Angeles: Tarcher.

Reason, P. (1993, September). Reflections on Sacred Experience and Sacred Science. *Journal of Management Inquiry, 2*(3), 273-283.

Reckmeyer, W. J. (1982). *The Emerging Systems Paradigm: An Historical Perspective.* Unpublished doctoral dissertation, The American University, Washington, DC.

Redfield, J. (1993). *The Celestine Prophecy.* Hoover, AL: Satori.

Redfield, J. (1996). *The Tenth Insight: Holding the Vision.* New York: Warner.

Rees, A. & Rees, B. (1961). *Celtic Heritage.* London: Thames & Hudson.

Reger, R. K., Mullane, J. V., Gustafson, L. T., & DeMarie, S. M. (1994, November). Creating Earthquakes to Change Organizational Mindsets. *The Academy of Management Executive, 8*(4), 31-46.

Reich, R. B. (1996, March 3). Cracks in the Economic Earth. *San Jose Mercury News,* p. C1.

Reisberg, B. (1995, October). In the Spirit of Business: Jewelry Company is for Spirit and Profit. *Psychic Reader,* p. 19.

Rheingold, H. (1994, February). PARC is Back! *Wired,* 91-95.

Rheingold, H. (1993). *The Virtual Community: Homesteading on the Electronic Frontier.* Reading, MA: Addison-Wesley.

Rhodes, L. (1989) The Un-Manager. In *INC. Guide to Managing People.* (pp. 166-179). New York: Prentice-Hall.

Richmond, B. (1990). Systems Thinking: A Critical Set of Critical Thinking Skills for the 90's and Beyond. *Proceedings of the 1990 International Conference on Systems Dynamics.* (Available from High Performance Systems, Inc.13 Dartmouth College Highway, Lyme, NH 03768).

Rinpoche, S. (1994). *The Tibetan Book of Living and Dying.* San Francisco: HarperCollins.

Roddick, A. (1991). *Body and Soul.* New York: Crown.

Roll-Hansen, J. (1962). *A Time for Trolls: Fairy Tales From Norway.* Oslo: Johan Grundt Tanum Forlag.

Roszak, T. (1992). *The Voice of the Earth: An Exploration of Ecopsychology.* New York: Simon & Schuster.

Rothschild, M. (1990). *Bionomics: Economy as Ecosystem.* New York: Henry Holt.

Rothschild, M. (1991, December). Call it Digital Darwinism. *Upside,* 3(10), 80-87.

Rothschild-Witt, J. (1979). The Collectivist Organization: An Alternative to Rational-Bureaucratic Models. *American Sociology Review, 44,* 509-527.

Ruether, R. R. (1992). *Gaia and God.* San Francisco: HarperCollins.

Ruether, R. R. (1983). *Sexism and God-Talk: Toward a Feminist Theology.* Boston: Beacon.

Rummler, G. A. & Brache, A. P. (1990). *How to Manage the White Space on the Organization Chart.* San Francisco: Jossey- Bass.

Sagan, C. (1973). *The Cosmic Connection: An Extraterrestrial Perspective.* Garden City, NY: Anchor.

Sahtouris, E. (1989). *Gaia: The Human Journey From Chaos to Cosmos.* New York: Pocket.

Sanday, P. R. (1981). *Female Power and Male Dominance.* Cambridge, MA: Cambridge University.

Sanford, J. A. (1980). *The Invisible Partners.* New York: Paulist.

Schaef, A. W. & Fassel, D. (1988). *The Addictive Organization.* San Francisco: Harper & Row.

Schaffer, B. (1994). *Down in the Valley.* Los Gatos, CA: Temblor.

Schecter, D. (1991). Beer's "Organizational Tensegrity: and the Challenge of Democratic Management. *Systems Practice, 4*(4), 303-317.

Schein, E. H. (1985). *Organizational Culture and Leadership.* San Francisco: Jossey-Bass.

Scheinin, R. (1995, October 14). Cosmic Angels: Physics Opens Windows to the Soul. *San Jose Mercury News,* pp. 1E, 9E.

Scheinin, R. (1994, November 5). Reinventing Ritual. *San Jose Mercury News,* pp. 1C, 11C.

Schumacher, E. F. (1973). *Small is Beautiful.* New York: Harper & Row.

Schwarz, J. (1980). *Human Energy Systems.* New York: Dutton.

Schwartz, P. & Ogilvy, J. (1979, April). *The Emergent Paradigm: Changing Patterns of Thought and Belief.* (VALS Research Report no. 7). Menlo Park, CA: SRI International.

Semler, R. (1989, September/October). Managing Without Managers. *Harvard Business Review,* 76-84.

Semler, R. (1993). *Maverick.* New York: Warner.

Semler, R. (1994, January/February). Why My Employees Still Work for Me. *Harvard Business Review,* 64-74.

Senge, P. M. (1990). *The Fifth Discipline.* New York: Doubleday.

Senge, P. M. (1990, Fall). The Leader's New Work: Building Learning Organizations. *Sloan Management Review,* 32(1), 7-23.

Senge, P. M., Roberts, C., Ross, R. B., Smith, B. J., & Kleiner, A. (1994). *The Fifth Discipline Fieldbook.* New York: Doubleday.

Sheldon, A. (1980, Winter). Organizational Paradigms: A Theory of Organizational Change. *Organizational Dynamics,* 61-79.

Sheldrake, R. (1988). *The Presence of the Past.* New York: Vintage.

Shine, J. (1996, June). Herd Mentality. *Wired,* 98-104.

Siegel, C. (1996, July-August). A New Declaration of Independence. *Utne Reader,* 51-54, 56.

Sigfried, T. (1996, January 1). Supersymmetry Could Impose Order Beyond Einstein's Vision. *The Dallas Morning News,* p. 7D.

Silvern, L. C. (1971). *Systems Engineering of Education: The Evolution of Systems* (2nd Ed.). Los Angeles: Education and Training Consultants.

Singer, E. A. (1957). *Experience and Reflection.* Philadelphia: University of Pennsylvania.

Singer, J. (1990). *Seeing Through the Visible World: Jung, Gnosis, and Chaos.* San Francisco: Harper & Row.

Slocombe, D. S.; Roelof, J. K.; Cheyne, L. C.; Terry, S. N. & den Ouden, S. (1993). *What Works: An Annotated Bibliography of Case Studies of Sustainable Development.* (Working paper no. 5). Sacramento, CA: International Center for the Environment and Public Policy.

Smith, A. (1975). *Powers of Mind.* New York: Random.

Smith, A. (1995, Spring). Virtue. *Story,* 43(2), 102-113.

Snell, M. B. (1995, July-August). Trials and Transformation. *The Utne Reader,* 62-70.

Snyder, G. (1983) *Axe Handles.* San Francisco: North Point.

Snyder, G. (1968). *The Back Country.* New York: New Directions.

Snyder, G. (1978). *Myths & Text.* New York: New Directions.

Snyder, G. (1992). *No Nature.* New York: Pantheon.

Snyder, G. (1965). *Riprap and Cold Mountain Poems.* Berkeley, CA: North Point.

Snyder, G. (1974). *Turtle Island.* New York: New Directions.

Spretnak, C. (Ed.) (1982). *The Politics of Women's Spirituality.* Garden City, NY: Anchor.

Starhawk (1993). *The Fifth Sacred Thing.* New York: Bantam.

Starhawk (1979). *Spiral Dance: A Rebirth of the Ancient Religion of the Great Goddess.* San Francisco: Harper.

Stata, R. (1989, Spring). Organizational Learning: The Key to Management Innovation. *Sloan Management Review,* 30(3), 63-74.

Steiner, C. M. (1981). *The Other Side of Power.* New York: Grove.

Stern, J. (Ed.) (1944). *The Complete Grimm's Fairy Tales.* (M. Hunt, Trans.) New York: Pantheon.

Stevens, B. (1970). *Don't Push the River.* Moab, UT: Real People.

Stewart, I. (1989). *Does God Play Dice? The Mathematics of Chaos.* Cambridge, MA: Blackwell.

Stewart, T. A. (1991, June). Brainpower. *Fortune, 123*(11), 44-46.

Stewart, T. A. (1992, May 18). The Search for the Organization of Tomorrow. *Fortune,* 92-98.

Stone, M. (1976). *When God Was a Woman.* San Diego: Harcourt Brace.

Stoppard, T. (1993). *Arcadia.* London: Faber & Faber.

Stroup, H. (1972). *Like a Great River: An Introduction to Hinduism.* New York: Harper & Row.

Swimme, B. (1985). *The Universe is a Green Dragon.* Santa Fe, NM: Bear.

Tannen, D. (1990). *You Just Don't Understand.* New York: Ballantine.

Tannenbaum, R., Margulies, N., Massarik, F., *et al.* (1987). *Human Systems Development.* San Francisco: Jossey-Bass.

Taylor, A. (1992). *Older Than Time: A Grandmother's Search for Wisdom.* London: Aquarian/Thorsons.

Templeton, K. H. (1996, March-April). Making the Transition to a World Without Work. *Open Exchange,* p. 85.

Thomas, R. R. (1991). *Beyond Race and Gender.* New York: American Management Association.

Thorsten, G. (1980). *God Herself: The Feminine Roots of Astrology.* Garden City, NY: Doubleday.

Tillich, P. (1966). *On the Boundary.* New York: Charles Scribner's Sons.

Toffler, A. (1990). *Powershift.* New York: Bantam.

Toms, M. (1994, Fall). Making Love Vibrant in the World: A Conversation with Andrew Harvey. *Common Ground,* 81, pp. 160-162, 170.

Trist, E. L. (1980). *The Evolution of Socio-Technical Systems: A Conceptual Framework.* Toronto: Ontario Quality of Work Life Centre, Ontario Ministry of Labour.

Trist, E. L., Higgin, G. W., Murray, H. & Pollack, A. B. (1963). *Organizational Choice.* London: Tavistock Institute.

Trzyna, T. C. & Osborn, J. K. (1995). *A Sustainable World: Defining and Measuring Sustainable Development.* Sacramento, CA: IUCN - The World Conservation Union.

Trzyna, T. C., Margold, E., & Osborn, J. K. (Eds.) (1996). (5th ed.) *World Directory of Environmental Organizations.* Sacramento, CA: International Center for the Environment and Public Policy.

Vaill, P. B. (1989). *Managing as a Performing Art.* San Francisco: Jossey-Bass.

Vaill, P. B. (1989, July 21). *Spirituality in the Age of the Leveraged Buyout.* Paper presented at the Conference on Spirituality in Life and Work, Georgetown University, School for Summer and Continuing Education, Washington, DC.

Valadez, S. E. & Valadez, M. (1992). *Huichol Indian Sacred Rituals.* Oakland, CA: Dharma Enterprises.

von Bertalanffy, L. (1968). *General Systems Theory.* New York: Braziller.

von Franz, M. L. (1972). *Problems of the Feminine in Fairy Tales.* Dallas: Spring.

von Oech, R. (1983). *A Whack on the Side of the Head.* New York: Warner.

Waldrop, M. M. (1992). *Complexity: The Emerging Science at the Edge of Order and Chaos.* New York: Simon & Schuster.

Walker, B. G. (1983). *Women's Encyclopedia of Myths and Secrets.* San Francisco: Harper.

Waterman, R. H. (1987). *The Renewal Factor.* New York: Bantam.

Waterman, R. H., Peters, T. J., & Phillips, J. R. (1980, June.) Structure is Not Organization. *Business Horizons,* 14-26.

Webster's New Twentieth Century Dictionary of the English Language. (1968). (2nd Ed.). Cleveland: World.

Weick, K. E. (1969). *The Social Psychology of Organizing.* Reading, MA: Addison-Wesley.

Weigand, D. (1996, March 10). Tracing the Coast Between Life and Death. *San Francisco Examiner & Chronicle: Book Review,* p. 3.

Weinberg, G. M. (1975). *An Introduction to General Systems Thinking.* New York: Wiley.

Weiner, N. (1948). *Cybernetics.* New York: Wiley.

Weiner, N. (1967). *Human Use of Human Beings.* New York: Doubleday.

Weisbord, M. R. (1989). *Productive Workplaces.* San Francisco: Jossey-Bass.

Wheatley, M. J. (1992). *Leadership and the New Science.* San Francisco: Berrett-Koehler.

White, W. F. & White, K. K. (1988). *Making Mondragon.* Ithaca, NY: Cornell.

Whiting, R. (1989). *You Gotta Have Wa.* New York: Vintage.

Wilber, K. (1980). *The Atman Project.* Wheaton, IL: Theosophical Publishing House.

Wilber, K. (1983). *Eye to Eye: The Quest for the New Paradigm.* Garden City, NY: Anchor.

Wilber, K. (Ed.) (1982). *The Holographic Paradigm and Other Paradoxes.* Boulder, CO: Shambhala.

Wilber, K. (1985). *No Boundary.* Boston: Shambhala.

Wilhelm, R. & Baynes, C. F. (1950). (Trans.) *The I Ching or Book of Changes.* Princeton, NJ: Princeton University.

Williams, R. H. (1989, July 16). Voyages in Space Lift Spirit Beyond Technology. *San Jose Mercury News: Arts and Books,* p. 22.

Windle, J. W. (1993). *True Women.* New York: Ivy.

Wing, R. L. (1982). *The Illustrated I Ching.* Garden City, NY: Doubleday.

Wolf, F. A. (1981). *Taking the Quantum Leap: The New Physics for Nonscientists.* New York: Harper & Row.

Yeager, J. & Rutan, D. (1987). *Voyager.* New York: Knopf.

Yi, C. (1988). *I Ching: The Tao of Organization.* (T. Cleary, Trans.). Boston: Shambhala.

Ywahoo, D. (1987). *Voices of Our Ancestors.* Boston: Shambhala.

Zimmerman, B. J. & Hurst, D. K. (1993, December). Breaking the Boundaries: The Fractal Organization. *Journal of Management Inquiry,* 2(4), 334-355.

Zohar, D. & Marshall, I. (1994). *The Quantum Society.* New York: William Morrow.

Zukav, G. (1979). *The Dancing Wu Li Masters.* New York: Bantam.

Zukav, G. (1989). *The Seat of the Soul.* New York: Simon & Schuster.

INDEX

Spirit, 11, 16, 22, 29, 40, 41, 43, 82, 93, 112, 114
 – community, 22
 – regaining, 101-102
 – team, 106
Spirituality, 46, 87, 115
Spontaneity, 22, 50, 80, 114, 120
Stability, 45, 46, 47, 61, 87, 108, 110
Star, 97-98. *See also* The Ringed Pentacle.
Status quo, 36, 38, 108, 118
Stewardship, 88
Story (ies), 11, 17, 30-32, 37, 52-55, 63, 80, 91, 93, 98, 107, 116, 124. *See also* Tales.
 – analysis of, 117-124
 – best of five, 95-100, 124
 – collective, 117, 124
 – five, 55-88. *See also* "Dance with Gaia;" "King of the Mountain;" "Magical Mystery Mime Troupe and Jazz Band," "Motocross;" "White Water Rafting."
 – ideal, 104-105, 117
 – life, 52, 53, 93, 103
 – system, 52-54, 107
 – your, 52, 53, 101, 102-105, 124
Storytelling, 32, 91, 93, 99
Strategist. *See* Individual shape, Strategist.
Strategy, 14, 26, 48, 68, 82, 96
Strengths, 18, 23, 73, 74, 86, 119, 122
 – build on, 110-116
 – collective, 92, 117
 – of "Dance with Gaia," 97
 – of five realities, systems, 92, 95, 97, 101, 110-115, 124
 – of "King of the Mountain," 96
 – of "Magical Mystery Mime Troupe and Jazz Band," 96-97
 – of "Motocross," 96
 – of "White Water Rafting," 96, 116
Stress, 14, 23, 24, 25, 34, 91, 103
Structure, 14, 27, 104
Success, 36, 46, 67, 81, 85, 96, 97, 111, 113, 115. *See also* Achievement.
 – critical elements for, 94-95
Sunny, 11, 17, 21-55, 91-101
Survival, 36, 42, 110, 111
 – of the fittest, 120
Sustainable society, 123
Symbol(s), 80, 97, 98, 117, 118, 119, 121, 122, 123
Synergy, 50, 99, 108
System(s), 5, 11-14, 17, 18, 33, 45, 49, 52, 53, 55, 84, 85, 87, 89, 98, 101
 – alternative(s), 14
 – best of five, 95-100, 124
 – challenge(s) of, *See* Challenge, central.
 – change of, *See* System change.
 – computer, 113
 – dysfunctional, 52, 107. *See also* Organization, unhealthy; Sandbox.

 – energy of, 109-110, 116
 – five, 13, 124
 – functional, 52. *See also* Organization, healthy; Wholesome system.
 – healthy, *See* Wholesome system.
 – information, 113, 114
 – intrusive, *See* Intrusive system.
 – life-support, 85
 – made me do it, 33
 – nervous, 89
 – organizational, *See* Organizational system.
 – self-organizing, 87, 114, 123. *See also* Gaia Hypothesis; Self-regulation.
 – solar, 86
 – strengths of, *See* Strengths.
 – weaknesses of, *See* Weaknesses.
 – wholesome, *See* Wholesome system.
System(s) change, 13-14, 17, 102, 107-124. *See also* Organizational change.
 – key considerations for, 108
Systems Theory, 25
Systems Thinking, 16, 18

Tales, 40, 55, 125. *See also* Story.
 – fairy, 21, 26, 30
 – of five realities, 57-88
Taliesin, 40
Tao Te Ching, 11, 89, 109
Tarot, 80, 82
Team, 23, 24, 51, 73, 112, 120
 – player, 12, 15, 78
Teamwork, 35, 74
Technology, 45, 48, 111, 113
Terminator, 67
Thinking, if-then, 45
Thoughts, 13, 94, 105. *See also* Creativity; Idea; Imagination; Innovation.
Tomlin, Lily, 57
Transformation, 17, 22, 36, 40, 42, 101, *See also* Change; Growth; Metamorphosis; Transition.
Transition, 42. *See also* Change; Growth; Metamorphosis. Transformation.
Transmigration, 40
Tribalism, 115, 122, 123
Trust, 45, 118, 121
Truth, 11, 14, 46, 53
Turbulence, 73, 74, 75, 112, 120. *See also* Change, rapid.
2001: A Space Odyssey, 85

Uncertainty, 26, 27. *See also* Chaos; Complexity.
Unconscious, collective, 40
Unifying threads, 117
 – in "Dance with Gaia," 123-124
 – in "King of the Mountain," 118
 – in "Magical Mystery Mime Troupe and Jazz Band," 122

THE AUTHOR

Susan M. Osborn, Ph.D., M.S.W., has a background that includes twenty-five years as a business and management consultant. She has also worked as an individual, group, and family therapist; parole agent; court supervisor; director of prison rehabilitation; editor; researcher; technical writer; professional organizer; career counselor; corporate trainer; performance management specialist; organizational development project manager; manager of compensation and benefits; and manager of human resource development.

She has taught at twenty different colleges and universities. After earning her doctorate in human and organizational systems she served as the director of a master's degree program in systems management. She is the senior author of *Assertive Training for Women* (1975) and lives in the San Francisco Bay Area.

Credit card orders call TOLL FREE
Rayve Productions
(800) 852-4890

24 HOURS   7 DAYS A WEEK

CALL AND ORDER NOW